They Don't Play My Music Anymore

How to Plan Your Future
When Your World Keeps Changing

Thomas W. McKee

D0048581

Advantage Point Systems, Inc.
Gold River, California

They Don't Play My Music Anymore

How to Plan Your Future
When Your World Keeps Changing

by Thomas W. McKee

Published by:

Advantage Point Systems, Inc.
11857 Old Eureka Way
Gold River, CA 95670 U.S.A.

ISBN: 1-928685-13-7
Library of Congress Catalog Card Number: 99-90356

Table of Contents

Appendix:
   Developing Your New Future Mission Statement
   Visioning Your Dream
   Personal Strategic Planning Retreat to Plan a Strategic Future
   SWOT Analysis

Preface

The book you are about to read is about transformational living. It is not merely about change, but it is about the transformation that goes on in our lives when we face change. It is through transformation that we change and grow.

I have outlined eight essentials of managing transitions. I need to stress, however, that by limiting myself to these eight elements of managing change, I am not suggesting that these are the only ones to be considered. There may be other steps that will help you manage the changes in your life. The eight essentials that form the core of this book are those that have personally guided my clients, friends and other successful people mentioned in the following pages to manage the transitions in their personal and professional lives. I also have found that these principles have guided me through dramatic changes.

On October 31, 1992, I was downsized, or as some might say, fired. I felt fear, anger and rejection. Because I was about to turn 51, I also experienced panic wondering just how up-to-date my skills were in this fast changing world. But that day has proven to be one of the best days of my life and on Halloween each year I like to celebrate this birth date of the new me. I had a dream for many years, but needed this crisis to make it happen. My business was conceived and born in the next few months and this book contains the many lessons I learned through this process. My company was incorporated in 1997 and I am proud to say that I have trained thousands of managers and supervisors for companies like Proctor and Gamble, The Money Store, the State of California, the Internal Revenue Service, and Pride Industries. I also have spoken for hundreds of associations and organizations on the subject of change.

I have given a lot of thought to how I can help you benefit most from the practical advice I offer. Because the topic of transformational living is so important, I have included several exercises in the appendix to help you plan for your future. These exercises are explained in the corresponding chapters in the book; therefore, they will not be as meaningful without reading the chapter.

I have a few final words to those of you who are facing a major career decision because you have been downsized, reorganized or reengineered. This is not a book on how to get a new job. Although the principles will help you prepare for that new job, the focus of this book is on developing your career, not your job. This book is about how to search within yourself and discover a new direction for the passion that lies deep within you. For some of you it may be a passion you have had for years but have not followed through. For others, you may be feeling the pain of rejection from being let go or reassigned and you are struggling to revive a passion you once had. For all of you, I believe this book can transform your life because I have been where you are, and have discovered a new passion for the career I now have.

I trust that as you study and apply the principles in this book, you will find the passion, knowledge, faith, hope and skills to successfully chart the course for your new future.

Thomas W. McKee

Acknowledgments

I am indebted to several people for helping me bring this project to completion:

To my wonderful wife, Susie, for her support and encouragement. Despite her incredibly busy schedule administrating and teaching graduate students at California State University, Sacramento, I kept leaving pages for her to look at as I tried to put my ideas down on paper. Her reactions and critique have been invaluable. But most of all, for over 35 years, Susie has encouraged and supported me when I was eager to pick up the baton of leadership and face a new piece of music when it would have been much easier for her if I had just tried to keep things as they were.

To my son Thom and his wife Amy, who have encouraged me to complete this dream that I have had for years. They not only kept asking me about it, but also have spent significant time proofing and editing the book. Without them this project would still be in my head rather than on paper.

To my clients, friends, family and organizations who have allowed me to tell stories on these pages. They include the following people:

Jan Nestler, executive director, the East Side Adult Day Services, Bellevue, Washington

Tug and Judy Miller, directors, National RV Park Institute, Auburn, California

Jon and Lori McKee, my son and daughter-in-law

Steve and Peggy King, owners, Mountain Jewel Ranch, Little Valley California

Mike and Linda Jones, owners, Rhapsody Inc., Cameron Park, California

Bach to the Beat of Sousa

> *Some Cat's Got It, Some Cat's Don't.*
> ♦ J.P. Richardson
> "The Big Bopper"

When the Big Bopper was asked what the secret of his success was, he answered "Some cats got it, some cats don't." I was sixteen when I first heard the Big Bopper say those intriguing words. As a teenager in the 1950's, the wild rock-n-roll music of Buddy Holly, Ritchie Valens and J.P. Richardson (more popularly known as the "Big Bopper") had entertained and inspired me. Driving in my hopped up '36 Ford the afternoon of the interview, I found myself puzzled by the Big Bopper's response. What did these cats have? Did I have it? I wanted to know exactly what some cats had that made them so successful. Within two months, I found out. What I learned that day was one of those life-changing lessons that has impacted the course of my life and has formed the framework of this book.

On a Tuesday morning, two weeks after the Big Bopper interview, I slipped into the Campbell High School band as usual – quiet, shy and unnoticed. Scrawled on the chalkboard were the words "Anyone who wants to try out for student director, write your name on the board." Eight names of popular students were jotted underneath. Seizing the moment, I walked to the board and wrote my name down.

As a high school sophomore, I had never assumed any role of leadership before. So, what motivated me – a rather vertically challenged, 5'4", average musician – to stand in front of the band and potentially risk my reputation? The answer was simple. I had practiced for this moment for five years. At the age of ten, I had spent countless hours leading an imaginary philharmonic band to John Philip Sousa's *Stars and Stripes Forever*. Tinker toy in hand, I would stand on a chair, cueing in the trombones, trumpets, clarinets, drums, flutes and piccolo as my parents' record player blared the tune. I knew every nuance, every entrance of a new instrument and every melody. When the band director announced that we could select our own music, I knew that my day had arrived.

The day arrived. As the eight students practiced their conducting skills to Sousa's tune, my confidence grew, pumping through my veins with each beat of the drum. Their performances were only mediocre. After what seemed like an eternity, I was handed the baton and strode to the podium. As I raised my baton, every instrument shot up in the air. I began to lead. To my delight, the band followed! The chemistry grew as I began cueing in different sections. I could see my quiet, reserved impression being transformed in the eyes of my fellow students. During measures of rest, I watched as students lowered their instruments and turned to each other saying "This guy is great!" And I was. When I had finished and my baton was lowered, I received a standing ovation and all but eight votes. I was the student director of the Campbell High School band. At that moment, I knew that I must be one of those cats that had it.

My life-changing moment came a few weeks later when Mr. Perkins, the bandleader, asked me to lead the band while he made a phone call. To my horror, I was asked to lead a Bach chorale, a piece I had never heard before. But an even bigger problem existed – I didn't know how to read music. I knew my own trumpet part, but I couldn't read bass clef, and the conductor's score looked like a jumble of black dots on the page. Gaining quick composure, I decided to follow the examples of many leaders faced with similar circumstances – fake it! Quickly, I counted the measures and arrived at 98. I determined to mentally count the measures out while leading the band, and when I reached 98, I would cut everyone off and no one would ever know the difference.

Standing before the band, I raised my baton and we were off…at John Philip Sousa's pace. Have you ever heard Bach to the beat of Sousa? The band had never sounded so bad. By the sixth measure, I lost count, and after ten feeble measures, I cut everyone off and said "Anyone for John Philip Sousa? It's all I know."

That is when I learned one of the most important lessons of my life. That is when I learned what some cats "got" and some cats don't. I began to understand that life was going to continue handing me new pieces of music and that I couldn't rely on old records forever to fake my way through. It was then that I learned that successful cats were leaders in their personal and professional lives. More specifically, I discovered that what some cats have and some cats don't is the ability to face any new piece of music. Life is going to be full of change. Success is the ability to read, interpret and manage those changes.   The same is true in our personal and professional lives. We must have the ability to stand before a new piece of music - any change - and know what to do.

First, the great conductor can read and interpret new music

Great conductors can look at a new score and immediately hear the symphony in their heads with all of the parts blending together. Musicians who know how to interpret all of those tiny black dots and lines on a new piece of music love to pick up a new score. Great conductors can feel the rhythm and make sense of the cacophony of musical instruments. They often pore over hundreds of musical scores before they pick the few that they are going to introduce to the band.

Just as the band leader has to interpret all of the parts of a score, we must be able to interpret the options and opportunities set before us. As we interpret each of these alternatives correctly, we can make better decisions about our future. Armed not only with basic knowledge and information about life, themselves and their industries, successful people know how to make sense of those elements—anticipating changes, keeping up with a rapid pace and making wise decisions along the way.

Second, the great conductor restores confidence by establishing a strong and clear beat

A skilled conductor sets a beat that is not only rhythmic, but also interpretive. When the conductor begins to lead, band members not only know what rhythm to play, but also when to crescendo and decrescendo, when to come in and go out and all the other subtleties and nuances that are involved in performing the piece. A poor conductor spells disaster! The team in transition needs a strong and interpretive beat from the team leader. Good leaders set the beat by helping their employees understand what their corporate culture is.

Facing a new piece of music is challenging. Learning new systems, cultures and technologies is disruptive; however, when a person has developed a system of learning, assimilating and organizing new information, he or she can often feel the new beat and establish a clear sense of direction.

Third, the great conductor breaks the score down into manageable sections

Too much at one time can be overwhelming. To deviate from the music analogy for a moment, consider Michael Jordan. When he returned to basketball after playing baseball for a while, Peter Vescy asked him, "Michael, do you think that you can come back to basketball where you left off - averaging 32 points a game?" Michael Jordan's response offers an incredibly valuable and insightful lesson. Michael Jordan said to Peter, "Why not? That's only eight points a quarter." By breaking the entire game down into sections, Michael Jordan could focus one quarter at a time. And he was successful.

What "some cats got" and "some cats don't" is the

ability to master these key personal leadership skills when they are faced with change. Like a great conductor, they can read and interpret the music, set an interpretive beat that others can follow, and break the music down into manageable parts. When these skills are applied, life's changing score can be met with confidence.

In 1959, Buddy Holly, Ritchie Valens, and The Big Bopper were tragically killed in a plane crash. Although gone physically, The Big Bopper's *Chantilly Lace* along with the music of Buddy Holly and Ritchie Valens lives on, especially in the hearts of many Baby Boomers. It has been many years since I learned what I call the "Big Bopper Lesson," but for the past 40 years I have built my career on what I learned as a 16-year-old. That is what this book is about. *They Don't Play My Music Anymore* is about interpreting and managing change in your personal and professional life.

Music for a New Millennium

A new millennium is ushering in a whole new work force. Downsizing, reengineering and reorganizations are leaving talented people without work. Many are at their prime earning power and are being left without promising options. Words like "free agency" and "self employed" are not just for the entrepreneur anymore. By the year 2010, some forecasters predict that 50% of the American workforce will be self-employed.[1]

What happens when you are facing a new piece of music

personally? Perhaps you are among the casualties of corporate downsizing, or perhaps you have had to face divorce or the death of someone close to you. Regardless of the change, your life has been thrown into an unwelcome transition that you didn't expect, plan for or desire. Nevertheless, the change has come and you are left standing before the world, holding the baton of personal leadership, staring at a new piece of music that is not only unfamiliar, but also very confusing and possibly even frightening. Most of all, you have absolutely no passion for this change. Perhaps you have lost all drive even to get out of bed in the morning. So, where do you go from here?

The following eight steps are essentials for interpreting these changes. When applied, they can help build confidence as you set a new beat that others can recognize and follow. Master these eight essentials and you will have a credible claim to face an unknown future. You will be an agent of change, not a victim.

Essential One:	Rediscover Your Passion
Essential Two:	Visualize Your Dream—the power of hope
Essential Three:	Manage the Five Phases of Culture Shock
Essential Four:	Increase Your Value with Intellectual Capital
Essential Five:	Focus Your Dream
Essential Six:	Think Strategically
Essential Seven:	Keep the Faith
Essential Eight:	Just Do It

[1] Allen Liff, "Future Think," *Association Management*, January 1998, p 40.

Essential One: Rediscover Your Passion
I Can't Hear the Music

> *A rock pile ceases to be a rock pile*
> *the moment a single man contemplates it,*
> *bearing within him the image of a cathedral.*
> ♦ Antoine de Saint-Exupery
> French novelist

Recently I was in a theater watching an adventure movie. While the movie only covered a few months of the main character's life, I was struck by the incredible excitement surrounding the lives of these characters on a daily basis. Each moment brought a new series of thrills as people dodged bullets, jumped off of buildings into speeding trucks and drove speedboats through flames of explosive fumes. But perhaps the most attention-grabbing element of the film (even more than the exciting action in the lives of the characters) was the music, a feature I have all too often taken for granted. For some reason on this particular evening, my hearing senses were more acute, and I became aware of the shaping power of the music on my own personal mood. When the characters were in danger, the music shifted to slow eerie tones. The tempo increased when characters were running for their lives. It became light and cheerful when people were laughing. And you could hear the melodic strings of the violin and cello crescendo as a love scene was introduced. With each decision the main character had to make, the music set the mood and walked him through the experience.

I began to think about the adventure, excitement and fun in my own life and I wondered what the soundtrack would play like. Certainly, life never is as exciting as an action-adventure film all of the time. We all have days when we wake up grumpy in the morning, the coffee doesn't taste as good and we feel a little unnoticed. But I dreamed on. If Weber and Rice were to write the soundtrack for my experiences in life, would it win an Oscar? As I was fantasizing about my personal soundtrack, I realized that it would contain periods of complete silence. When I have had the rug pulled out from under me, I feel as if the soundtrack suddenly becomes deathly silent.

I don't hear any music sometimes. It's as if I'm standing in the shower in Janet Leigh's place, unaware of the killer lurking on the other side of the curtain. Hitchcock was a master at creating mood through music and silence. In the famous death scene in *Psycho*, the only sound heard as the killer slowly approaches Janet Leigh is the sound of water in the shower. I remember jumping out of my seat the first time I saw that famous death scene. Why did I jump? I jumped because the screeching music broke through the silence. When silence occurs for a prolonged period of time, we often find ourselves jumping at any music, good or bad, simply because it has broken through the silence that we've settled into.

As I have spoken with thousands of people over the years, I have discovered that many people caught in the midst of transition often don't hear any music at all. Paralyzed with fear, or perhaps numbed after prolonged silence, they have lost their passion to even get out of bed in the morning. And when they do rouse themselves to finally pull back the covers and crawl out, it certainly isn't to the beat of any exciting music. Have you ever felt afraid of a silent score, wondering if a killer was lurking just out of reach?

Why do you get out of bed in the morning? Recently, I asked this question at a teambuilding retreat. One of the participants, Beverly, stopped the conversation cold and confronted each of us by saying, "Tom, I hate that question. I hate it when people like you ask us to discover our passion. I don't know why I get out of bed. I would like to come up with some great answer, but I usually get out of bed because I have to get the kids off to school, go to work, or many times, just because I have to go to the bathroom. That is a stupid question!"

Maybe you are bothered by this question too. I am sure that others at the retreat felt the same way Beverly did, but may not have stated their feelings so boldly. Beverly had lost her passion for life. She no longer heard any music in life. Her soundtrack had stopped.

What Beverly was experiencing in her life is what I call the survival mode of living. Survival mode is when you get out of bed in the morning because you "have" to and not because you "want" to. Tragically, many people find themselves trapped in the survival mode of living and consequently lead unfilled and unfulfilled lives. I have been there. We all have been there. It is a part of life that none of us enjoy very much. But in order to embrace change with a sense of hope and passion, we must be able to move out of our survival mode into a transformational mode. If we don't, the burden will intensify and we will end up feeling hopeless and discouraged.

The survival mode of life is a necessary component of our daily lives. Like its name implies, it assists us with basic survival. It includes the normal changes that happen in the common activities of personal development. But there's more to this life than just surviving! That's where the transformational mode of life comes in. Transition is the go-between between just getting by in the survival mode, and living the exciting and fulfilling life you've always dreamed of in the transformational mode. During periods of uncomfortable transition, we must recognize that life doesn't have to be a rut, but that it can be more. Such thinking leads us to the transformational mode, which encompasses the dramatic changes that occur through the revolutionary activities of development. Notice the choice of words: dramatic (drama) and revolutionary (revolution). To many, these words are frightening. But they don't have to be. They can be words of excitement and hope. Change doesn't have to be a four-letter word.

Two analogies help to understand the difference between survival and transformational living: School Daze and Home Improvement.

School Daze

Picture yourself in your high school days. What motivated you to get out of bed in the morning? Maybe it was Mom or Dad, but whatever the external impetus, you rolled out of bed and went to class to survive. In the process of attending classes, your knowledge increased and you were challenged to grow and stretch. But while you sat in class, another activity was occurring. You were discovering your own personal role. As it developed and you played your part, everyone in the class came to know you by that role. Perhaps you were the campus athlete, clown, brain, nerd, beauty queen or jerk. Regardless of your personal role, you discovered your own mode of survival, and you learned and grew within a role that you personally owned and felt comfortable in.

In contrast to the survival mode of life is the transformational mode. Lori Bard had an identity in high school that contributed to her security and significance. She was a cheerleader, ice skater, swimmer and excellent student. Her family did not have the money to send her to a university and like many 18-year olds, she wanted to venture out on her own rather than stay at home and go to the local community college. The only way she could see that happening was to join the Air Force. She packed up her identity and moved from Phoenix to Texas to enter boot camp.

Lori's first week in boot camp was one of the most difficult weeks in her entire life. Not only was she being pushed physically and psychologically, she was far from the things that made up her previous identity. After a couple of days of being screamed at by several of the Air Force's stern drill instructors, the girls in Lori's flight were allowed to make one two-minute phone call. All fifty girls lined up at the phones and called home in turn. As Lori stepped up to the phone to call her mother, her drill instructor stood behind her with a stopwatch which was already started. As soon as her mom answered, Lori immediately broke down in tears and said, "Mom, please get me out of here. Do whatever you can, just get me out of here!" (Later she found out that this was the same thing that most of the other girls had said during their phone calls.) Standing before a new world, Lori didn't like what she saw at first. Her new world was a scary place. In the midst of incredible transition, a transformation was occurring. No longer did she get up and go to high school classes and activities. She moved across the country, saw new faces and strange places, and found that life was not the comfortable little box that she had grown accustomed to. Her high school roles were no longer recognizable to most. She lost a little bit of the identity she had formed, and began a transforming process – a process of becoming.

Eventually, Lori overcame her fears and became a squad leader. At the end of her nine weeks of bootcamp she was the honor graduate of her flight. She then went on to technical school and graduated with honors again. Finally she passed her CDC's with honors receiving what few Air Force enlisted men and women have achieved, and graduated with triple honors.

At first Lori had felt overwhelmed without her old roles to support her. She had been stripped of her security and significance. But as she developed new friends and new skills, her confidence and comfort began to grow. She was trained as a medical technician, worked with doctors and nurses, and began to find a new identity in the medical field. She joined a local church and met new friends. When transferred to Mather Air Force Base in Sacramento, she spent the weekends skiing in Lake Tahoe, traveling to San Francisco and going on activities with the church college and career group. It was there that Lori met my son Jonathan, and shortly thereafter they were married. Lori had experienced transformation.

Transformation is the psychological time of letting go of the past and beginning again. With each new transformational journey we embark on, we take knowledge and wisdom gained from past experience, apply it to new situations and expand and explore into new areas of thinking, believing and acting. The transformational mode of life is a time of discovering a new passion. It is a time of creativity and development, and should be a time filled with hope. However, when we allow fear to dominate during times of inescapable change and transition, the joy of the journey can be lost, transformation stagnated and we may find ourselves slipping into the rut of survival mode living.

The most dramatic changes take place through the transformational mode of living. It is a rite of passage in which a radical departure from former ways of thinking and doing takes place. If we allow it, change can be an agent of hope and excitement, putting an end to the old patterns of the survival mode and ushering in new strategies to excel in the transformational mode. Push out of your mind for a moment the subtle thoughts of inadequacy that may be creeping in. Thoughts like "I'm not good at change," and "I like things the way they are" need to be replaced by feelings of competency and enthusiasm. Change is inevitable. While it may seem intimidating, it never needs to be threatening. In fact, change is a sign of life. At its core, life necessitates change. Without change, there is stagnation and ultimately death. Our challenge is to seek to capture and comprehend change from the chaos of the surrounding culture and be able to utilize it in transformational ways.

It is easy to get in a rut in the survival mode of living. We are comfortable within the roles we have adopted and the school environments we are familiar with. But all of a sudden we graduate and move out of our homes and into new towns and go off to college. Many of us have experienced this transformational mode when we were 17 or 18 years old. We moved into a new community, sometimes thousands of miles away, leaving behind our homes, families, friends and roles. For many of us, the first few days away from home were some of the scariest days of our lives, not because we were threatened by real killers, but because we feared the unknown.

Situations like these illustrate the transforming power of change in our lives. They are periods in which we are stripped of all our former roles. While we are establishing new identities, we are just a name or a number in the computer. We may feel momentarily off balance, unstable and fragmented. In such times, our values and principles determine how we will respond. How do we deal with these changes? Do we fear the unknown so much that we remain paralyzed? If so, the idea of change most likely brings to mind memories of fear, pain, frustration, and isolation. Or, do we view the transitions as a necessary part of the transforming process and allow ourselves to broaden our perspective? If so, the idea of change is an exciting one, beginning with the initial uneasiness of culture shock and gradually giving way to feelings of competency and enjoyment.

Home Improvement

The second analogy that illustrates the difference between survival mode and transformation mode of living is "home improvement." Most people clean their house on a weekly basis. This is survival mode living. We vacuum and dust and pick up the house. We wash windows several times a year. But one day, we decide we are tired of our home, so we remodel. We go in and tear out the kitchen and add a family room.

Some years ago, when my wife, Susie, and I remodeled our home, it was total chaos. The transition from survival mode to transformational mode was unbelievable. We had been told it was going to be bad, but the stories we heard were not even close to the upheaval we went through. We ate dust for weeks as we cooked in a microwave in our bathroom. When the project was done, it was wonderful. But the disorder we went through was "transformational living" at its core.

There are three types of people in this world: those that love the finished product and are willing to wade through the messy transitional periods (these people have beautiful homes); those who hate the transitions so much that they're willing to stay in the status quo (these people haven't remodeled since the seventies); and those who can't seem to make up their mind and constantly fluctuate between change and stagnation, never reaching any final product (these people have disheveled homes "under construction" at all times). What does your house look like? Do you hate the smell of wet paint and the taste of sawdust in your coffee? Does your dislike for chaos and your desire for orderliness and continuity prevent you from renovating rooms? Or do you visualize the final product and enjoy the chaos of the moment? What happens when we adventure into a transformational mode of living? We begin to develop and act out new passions. When we were remodeling our home, it was exciting chaos. Sure, it was a mess. But every day when I came home, I was excited to see what was done. Every morning when I got out of bed, I was excited to see what the new day brought. Granted, my sons kept wishing for an Amish barn-building day, but the process of remodeling our kitchen was a little lengthier and a lot more chaotic.

Are you in survival mode? Have you lost your passion? Would you love to restore that passion? Perhaps you need to take the leap from the survival mode into the transformational mode. Maybe you are being forced to take this leap and the process is filled with fear and resentment. But regardless of the force behind the change, it must be bridged. Change is inevitable.

Feeling Passionless?

I remember vividly the day I lost all my passion. I felt so defeated that I could not have even answered the question, "What is your passion?" I had been hired to help start a new company. The whole process energized me, and for two years I worked night and day, making next to nothing in an attempt to get this company off the ground. But the company was not making it. I realized that in the next few months I would probably lose my job. I had always been successful, and in an attempt to suppress the growing reality of pending joblessness, I refused to believe that we would fail. The fateful day arrived. On Halloween, a Friday evening, as I was packing up to go home to several hundred trick-or-treaters, my boss called me in and let me go. For the moment, I was out of a job.

I was devastated. As I walked out of that office and went home, I felt drained, defeated, and exhausted after two years of tireless work. But, most of all, I felt rejected. In addition to my passionless feelings, I went home to an empty house that night. My wife, Susie, was out of town for the weekend, and I was left to man the door and attempt to be cheerful. It worked for about the first 20 trick-or-treaters. Finally, after about 15 minutes of distributing candy to our neighborhood children, I turned off the front light, went into my bedroom, turned on the TV and ate every single one of those tiny Snickers bars. I don't know how many I ate. All I know is that I ate them all and I got terribly sick.

The next day, after I went for a long walk and got over the chocolate hangover, I began the process of outlining the business that has restored my passion, given me a new sense of hope, encouragement and inspiration, and has culminated in the development of this course. It dawned on me that change was a force that was inescapable. But as I looked around me in my immediate family as well as in the surrounding community and world, I realized that many people were simply existing, devoid of passion and hope, surviving day to day, sometimes minute to minute. They had lost sight of the joys of life and yielded to a pattern of existence that would get them out of bed, their kids dressed and to school, their dinners on the table, and around it went.

I had found myself in this same mode. The epiphany of the moment gave me a new sense of hope and direction. But I must be honest. While I felt some immediate reenergizing as I outlined my basic goals, the energy soon gave way to frustration as I struggled for a few months to construct my new future. I felt like a giant rug had been pulled out from under me, and I didn't know exactly how or where to stand. Was I going to step on another rug only to have it yanked out again? I didn't like the uncertainty. I was in a period of transition. But what I didn't realize was the exciting future that awaited me. For the moment, I felt lost and passionless. I realized that I couldn't be in survival mode for long. I had been thrust into a transition that I wasn't prepared for. Despite occasionally overwhelming feelings of gloom, I decided to be an optimist and look to my future with hope.

The next steps are those I followed to help me discover my passion. But a critical ingredient for success must be stated here. In order to even begin exploring my passions, I had to be in the transformational mode. When we enter the transformational mode, it is like letting go of one trapeze and looking for the next one to appear. I didn't know when my next trapeze would come, and I felt like I was hanging in midair with no safety net. There were days when I had a hard time getting up in the morning with feelings of excitement. But, the beautiful part of the transformational process is that those were also times when I began to discover the process of restoring my passion.

You may be in one of three places in your life. You may have a passion that you have never followed. You are tired of survival mode living and are ready to let go of one trapeze and move into transformational mode. Your passion is just an idea, and at times you want to take the risk. The next essentials are a way to map out your plan to follow your passion.

You may also find yourself in the place where I was – in that in-between period. The day that I was let go from my job turned out to be the beginning of an exciting period of my life. I began the process of discovering a hidden passion of mine and learning how to develop that passion in a free agency market.

Or, you may be in a period of stability, comfortable within your roles, responsibilities and environment. In this environment, you feel confident and competent to handle chaos within established and experienced boundaries. But the idea of change may feel intimidating. If there is one thing that I can convey in this book, it is that change will happen. If you are presently in a "stable" situation, expect that things will change, but don't be afraid of the process. This book is designed to inspire the passionless, direct the discouraged and equip the comfortable to face changes as they occur.

The experiences I went through during those few ensuing months after losing my job have produced the general outline of this book. They have also formed the content of our workshop entitled "Facing a New Piece of Music in Your Personal Life." I have experienced firsthand the importance of these essentials in facing change and what it means to be an agent of change rather than a victim. The result of stepping out of survival mode into transformational mode is that power is unleashed and we are able to face any new piece of music or circumstance in life. How does this happen?

- We must have hope.
- We must manage the transition phases.
- We must increase our value with intellectual capital.
- We must focus that hope into a new future.
- We must think strategically about the future.
- We must have faith when in doubt.
- We must act on our hope, strategy and faith.
- We must return to the first essential and become passionate about our future!

Essential Two: Visualize a Picture of Hope

> *In rejecting change, we often*
> *cheat ourselves of the quest.*
> ◆ Rachel Naomi Remen, M.D.

If there was one gift I could give to everyone going through transition, it would be hope. But I can't give hope. Hope is something that comes from within. It is like motivation. Motivation is an inside activity. Hope is the expression of our dreams. It looks to the future and asks, "Why not?"

In March, 1972, I picked up the mail and found the latest issue of *Life* magazine.[1] I scanned the pictures quickly as I walked into the house. An article seemed to leap off the page. I read it and reread it, and as I did, my thinking was permanently transformed. The story was about a young man, John Goddard, who at the age of fifteen set down 127 goals. By age 47, he had achieved 103 of them. The goals were listed by category and there was a check mark by each one he had achieved.

As a fifteen-year-old, he had heard his parents and grandparents say so often, "I wish I had done that." He did not want to ever say those words, so his list included many of the rivers he wanted to explore, such as the Nile, Amazon, Congo,

---

Colorado, Yangtze and Niger. He included the mountains he wanted to climb, including Everest, McKinley, Kilimanjaro, Ararat, Kenya, Cook, Matterhorn, Rainier, Fuji, Vesuvius and the Grand Tetons.

He also wanted to carry out a career in medicine, visit every country in the world, study Navajo and Hopi Indians, learn to fly an airplane, retrace the travels of Marco Polo and Alexander the Great and ride a horse in the Rose Parade.

His list goes on to include the following: become an Eagle Scout; dive in a submarine; ride an elephant, camel, ostrich and bronco; play flute and violin; make a parachute jump; go on a church mission; study native medicines and bring back useful ones; bag camera trophies of elephant, lion, rhino, cheetah, cape buffalo, and whale; learn to fence; learn jujitsu; teach a college course; watch a cremation ceremony in Bali; explore the sea depths; write a book; publish an article in *National Geographic* magazine; learn French, Spanish and Arabic; read the Bible from cover to cover; read the works of Shakespeare, Plato, Aristotle, Dickens, Thoreau, Rousseau, Hemingway, Twain, Burroughs, Talmage, Tolstoi, Longfellow, Keats, Poe, Bacon, Whittier and Emerson (not every work of each); become proficient in the use of a plane, motorcycle, tractor, surfboard, rifle, pistol, canoe, microscope, football, basketball, bow and arrow, lariat, and boomerang; play Clair de Lune on the piano; watch a fire-walking ceremony (in Bali and Surinam); milk a poisonous snake; light a match with a .22-caliber rifle; circumnavigate the globe (four times); land on and take off from an aircraft carrier; marry and have children (has five).

In 1972, all of these had been accomplished. By 1972, he

only had 30 countries left to visit. By the time John Goddard had reached his 47th birthday, he had accomplished all but two dozen of his life goals. And the fallout of all of this was that in 1972, he was earning as much as $50,000 a year as an adventurer-lecturer (not bad in 1972 dollars).

I sat down and felt exhausted after reading the list. I was 31 years old and felt that I had let so much of life slip away. I had never been out of the United States, except for one-day trips to Canada and Mexico. I decided that things needed to change. My wife, Susie, and I sat down with a piece of paper and asked ourselves, "What are 50 things we would like to do before we die?" We had two small preschool boys and wondered what kind of example we would give to them.

Our list included graduate school, travel and work in Africa, Europe, enough money in the bank for our boys to attend private universities, and on and on. Susie, a high school English teacher, wanted to go to graduate school and become a university professor – today she is a tenured professor.

Never Be Afraid to Dream!

What do you want to do? What is your vision? I believe that successful outcomes originate as dreams and ideas in our imagination. Creative brainstorming is the fountain of imagination. Interpreting a new piece of music is not just learning, but it is taking our knowledge and vision of hope and being creative with it. It is being innovative.

When Phil Knight started his athletic shoe business in 1964, he named it Nike for the Greek goddess of victory because he was building an innovative product to help people win – not just a shoe. Knight took an item that everyone else was taking for granted and turned it into one of the most popular icons in the world. Like Henry Ford, Phil Knight was a dreamer. Ford's dream was to put a car in everyone's garage. He did. And Knight put a Nike on every foot. Like Knight and Ford, dreams can be turned into focused visions that lead to successful outcomes.

The Juice Guys, two young college graduates, have another exciting story that all began with an idea of creating a juice company. What began as an innovative dream in 1989 materialized to over 100 employees and established markets in over 30 states and international territories in Canada, Europe, Korea and South and Central America. Tom Scott and Tom First, the Juice Guys, in only eight years owned a $30 million-and-growing juice company, Nantucket Nectars. [2]

Rev. Steve King is a visionary who wears cowboy boots, a ten-gallon hat, and sits tall on his registered Morgan stallion, "Tuffy," as he rides over his 900-acre ranch early each morning to check on the cattle. Mountain Jewel Ranch is no ordinary ranch. It is a licensed adult residential facility. The ranch hands are developmentally disabled adults who enjoy spending their mornings working odd jobs such as chopping wood, mowing lawns, feeding animals and haying. They raise beef cattle and Morgan horses and grow hay on 900 acres in beautiful Little Valley in the northeastern corner of California. The ranch boasts about 60 head of cows and 400 tons of grass hay each summer. Steve raises Morgan horses and also has a team of Belgians named "Buck" and "Dolly." Most of the "ranchers" – adults with disabilities – have animal projects,

[2] Sean Flynn, "Beverage Isle," *Boston Magazine,* March 1997.

and participate in the raising of pigs, rabbits, chickens, a donkey and a ewe.

Thirteen years ago I was riding horseback with Steve and Peggy King over the undeveloped ranch. It was scattered with old buildings, heaps of trash and broken fences. But Steve saw something more. He looked out on the undeveloped land and imagined a working ranch, a growing head of cattle, bunkhouses, a ranch house, a cookhouse and a recreation room. As he and his wife, Peggy, envisioned a new and exciting future, they realized that there would be many obstacles to overcome before reaching their destination. So, one by one, they slowly added buildings and facilities to their property which were constructed mostly with materials donated by people in their community and with free labor set up by churches and community groups. They also experienced some terrible setbacks, including a fire that destroyed one of their bunkhouses and a dam that broke on their property. But these trials were overcome and today, Mountain Jewel Ranch is a living dream come true.

The dream goes back about 30 years when Steve and Peggy's second son, Russ, was born and diagnosed with Down's Syndrome. Through the years, Steve and Peggy have developed a passion for the families of developmentally disabled adults. As a minister of a small church, Steve had connections to many missionary families who were struggling with how to care for their adult disabled children. Raised in Bend, Oregon, Steve had grown up loving horses. Even as a college student in Los Angles, he kept a horse in his backyard. His passion for the developmentally disabled and his love for horses came together when he and Peggy established Mountain Jewel

Ranch.

What are your dreams? What are your ideas? What is your passion? What would you really like to be doing? Tom Scott and Tom First, on a yacht for two weeks, visualized Nantucket Nectars. Steve King, while riding Tuffy, visualized a working ranch for adults with disabilities. Get away from life's stressors. Go to your favorite place. Is it the beach? Is it the mountains? Is it along a river near your home? Wherever it is, take some time to get away and follow this simple exercise to help you set some far-reaching goals:

1. Take 30 uninterrupted minutes and write down at least 30 things that you want to do before you die. Try for 50 if you can. Think of educational desires, physical, vocational, recreational, spiritual, financial, family, etc.

2. Pick the top 5 and prioritize them.

3. Place a "$" sign by each one that will cost money to accomplish. Ask how much.

4. Place an "S" (to indicate support) by each one in which you feel you have the encouragement and support from the significant people in your life (spouse, family, friends, etc.).

5. Place a "V" next to any that are visionary in your estimation.

The above steps are brainstorming exercises to stimulate visionary thinking. Your mind is full of ideas. It is estimated that over 2000 messages enter our brains each day. It is not that we don't have a lot of ideas; it is that we are so overloaded with ideas that we cannot sort them out. We find ourselves trapped like the person who says, "I've got a photographic memory...my trouble is that I have no film." The brainstorming process is a method to get the ideas organized and out in the open.

Essential Three: Manage Culture Shock

> *An adventure is only an inconvenience*
> *rightly understood.*
> *An inconvenience is only an adventure*
> *wrongly understood.*
> ◆ C.K. Chesterton

Workers experience culture shock when transition occurs just like people do when they move to a foreign country. In their transition, they encounter five stages of culture shock. Oftentimes, government workers, international company employees and missionaries go through globalization training before they make such a move in order to more smoothly bridge and prepare for the changes about to take place. They learn how to proactively manage the five stages of culture shock. Like never before, companies and individuals who are experiencing the swift upheaval caused by downsizing, rightsizing or reengineering must become culture shock experts by learning to recognize and manage the following five phases.

Tourist

Phase One: Tourist
Restoring a Passion for Adventure

The Tourist is an outsider looking in. Tourists live out of suitcases and keep comparing their home culture to the culture of the country they are visiting. Often this comparison is degrading and condescending. In a completely foreign culture it can also be somewhat threatening.

Tourists look at change as only temporary. They know that "things will get back to normal" and consequently have no motivation to unpack and move in. When companies experience transition, this phase can extend for too long. It is a comfort zone for many. While this is natural, the wise team leader understands the importance of moving to Phase Two. People can get stuck in Tourist mode which can lead to denial of the actual transition. When correctly approached, Phase One is an adventure launching pad – a time of planning and excitement. The best way to deal with this phase is to be proactive about the changes rather than reactive to them, or worse yet, inactive. People who are planning the trip are much more likely to build better options than those who hang on to see what happens.

My oldest son became a Tourist when he went off to college in Minnesota. Having just spent a summer in the sunny mountains of Santa Cruz with weekday surfing excursions and evening campfires by the beach, the cold Minnesota weather thrust him into immediate culture shock. Rather than taking an interest in the sights and activities that his new environment had to offer, he quickly digressed to talking about California, thinking about California, doodling in his school notes about California and simply annoying all of his roommates, friends and casual acquaintances with his nostalgia for his home state. In the process, he alienated himself and missed out on incredible opportunities like ice skating, building snow castles, ice fishing, attending the Garrison Keillor show, seeing plays in Minneapolis and building relationships with Minnesotans and other students from around the country and world. After several months of misery, he decided to try "unpacking" his suitcase, accepting his new home environment and attempting to meet new people and experience new activities. It was then that he moved into the next phase.

People undergoing change in companies or organizations face the same quandary. Recently, I was leading a three-day workshop for a California State agency. They had reorganized their department into "cross-functional" teams so that they could better serve their customers. As a part of that reorganization, I was hired to teach the entire staff of over 550 managers/supervisors, team leaders and team members how to work in a "cross-functional" team rather than a hierarchical organization. It was exciting to see the enthusiasm that most of the people shared for the change and their eagerness to participate in the three-day workshop. We broke the department down into groups of 25 people, so the training process took around 21 weeks to complete.

But in each training session I found some Tourists. They refused to unpack their suitcases and remained very critical of the whole change process. As I listened to most of their reasons, I came to the conclusion that they were afraid of the next zone – the Foreigner Phase. If they accepted the change, they felt that they would lose the security and significance of their old position. And that was just too much for them to handle. They chose to remain in a critical, outsider Tourist Phase and hoped the new organization would fail so they would not have to change and risk the loss of their comfort zone.

I remember visiting some friends on a military base in Europe. I was amazed to find American service personnel who had rarely been off base, except when required to. They lived on base, did all of their shopping in the commissary on base, enjoyed movies, dining and other forms of entertainment on base and all of their friends were other military families who spent their time on base. They were living in the center of one of the most dramatic and colorful historical sights in the world, and they never ventured out. Others, however, risked the discomfort of new surroundings and explored the exciting culture. They formed strong and lasting friendships with beautiful memories that cannot be erased. Some twenty years later, they continue to write old friends and visit. By accepting the new culture, they gained rich experiences. Those of us facing transition need to make the same adjustment.

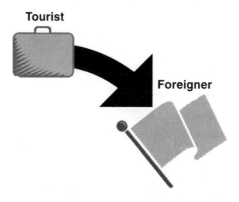

Phase Two: Foreigner
Restoring Hope

As soon as travelers unpack their suitcases and realize that they are going to be living in new territory for a while, they quickly move into the Foreigner Phase. A passion for adventure can be diminished if team members don't move through this phase quickly. It is in this stage when people lose their sense of significance and security. Academic degrees, accomplishments and past positions of leadership often are not recognized in a new setting. People feel as though they are starting over again. Like the foreigner in a new culture who must learn a new language and build new relationships, the worker in a downsized and reengineered culture must learn new terms and adjust to a new position on a new work team. Workers often feel that they have lost their turf and team membership. The Foreigner Phase can be a crisis phase, and nothing can destroy morale more quickly than eroding the foundation of security.

The Foreigner Phase is a very difficult time for most, but it is also an exciting time. People in this phase are experiencing the transitional mode of living (Chapter 1). When my daughter-in-law, Lori, went off to bootcamp, she unpacked her suitcase and lost all of her significance and security. How did she get through that transition? How do the members of a work team going through reorganization and reengineering get through this transition? When I lost my job that gave me security and significance, how did I get through this transition? The answer can be found through the experiences of a man named Viktor E. Frankl. He found himself in a foreign place that would have stripped most of us of our security and significance if we had been in his shoes.

Viktor E. Frankl, a psychiatrist from Vienna, spent three years at Auschwitz and interned at other Nazi prisons. Out of his experiences in those prison camps he wrote *Man's Search for Meaning*. In his book, Frankl says that the Nazis could strip him down to naked existence, but the one thing they could not take from him was the attitude with which he chose to respond to each and every situation. Ponder for a moment the impact of this statement. Picture Frankl in a concentration camp, stripped to naked existence, having lost his family, all his belongings, and forced to dig with his bare hands in the frozen ground for food. It is almost unimaginable. Yet, Frankl says of the situation:

We who lived in concentration camps can remember the men who walked through the huts comforting others, giving away their last piece of bread. They may have been few in number, but they offer sufficient proof that everything can be taken from a man but one thing: the last of the human freedoms—to choose one's own attitude in any given set of circumstances, to choose one's own way.[1]

Frankl discovered that the one thing his captors could not take away from him was his right to choose his attitude. Consequently, he was freer than his guards who seemed imprisoned by Nazi propaganda and shackled by the cruel and heartless orders given at the whim of the Nazi regime.

Recently, Susie and I traveled to Germany to spend time with some friends. On our trip, we visited the concentration camp where Frankl was imprisoned. The experience was incredibly moving and prompted me to reread Frankl's book. As I did, I became personally challenged to recommit myself to some of Frankl's conclusions. Namely, I wanted to choose how I would respond. I wanted to be in control of my attitude regardless of the circumstances around me.

On our flight home, we arrived in San Francisco to catch a commuter flight to Sacramento. We passed quickly through customs and were waiting for our flight when we discovered that all commuter flights were an hour late. I decided that the situation was OK – I was still in charge of my attitude. As soon as I had chosen my positive attitude, we heard an announcement that the plane would be another hour late. After two more announcements and four more hours of delay, I had forgotten Frankl's advice entirely and was casting aspersions

[1] Viktor E. Frankl, *Man's Search for Meaning,* Pocket Books, New York, 1959, p 104

on the airline, the pilots, the weather and anybody I could think of. Struggling with jetlag, fatigue and general discomfort, the situation was compounded when we arrived in Sacramento. It was mid-June and Sacramento had been hit with 50-mile-an-hour winds. Most of the power lines had blown down. Very few of the stoplights were working between the airport and home. We sat in our car for another couple of hours, inching our way home – a home we had not been in for almost a month.

In the midst of my discomfort and complaining, I happened to remember Frankl's definition of freedom: "Ultimate freedom is man's right to choose his attitude." As I sat in my air-conditioned car, I realized that I had not chosen my attitude but I was in bondage to my circumstances. They were situations that were outside of my control. I felt ashamed and discouraged thinking of Frankl under conditions of intense cruelty, hunger, loneliness, grief and oppression. But there was a commonality between us – we both were dealing with situations outside our control. He had chosen to respond positively. I had chosen to respond in anger and frustration.

Separating the Problems from the Givens

There are things we can control in life and things that we cannot. So much of the anxiety we experience in our lives is a result of being stressed out by things we cannot control – things like airplanes, winds and stoplights. Things that we can control can be considered "problems." For example, I have a weight problem but I do not have a height problem. There is something I can do about my weight, but there is nothing I can do about my height. When I was 16, I felt that I had a height problem. I was waiting for my growth spurt. I am still waiting for my growth spurt, but my height no longer bothers me. At 15 – even at 21 – it bothered me. But one day I realized that I could do nothing about my height. It wasn't a problem. It was a given. Frankl lived this lesson in prison. Most of his decisions were not his. But the one thing he could control was how he would respond. And he considered this the greatest freedom that we as human beings possess.

If we can learn to recognize the uncontrollable situations in life as givens, approach them with attitudes of acceptance, determine the controllable problems around us, and seek ways to exert power and influence over them, we can experience tremendous freedom. This doesn't just apply to life's small things like airplanes, winds and stoplights, but it can impact our thinking even in situations that seem overwhelmingly out of our hands (such as Viktor Frankl's experiences in concentration camps). We do not have to be victims. We have the power to choose to be free by choosing how we respond. We can be free by choosing to change the things we can, like our weight, hair color or coffee selection while choosing our attitude about the things we cannot control, like our height, health status (in some instances), and the response of others to us.

In addition to choosing our own attitude while in the Foreigner Phase, we can get through this stage by moving to the next phase as quickly as we can.

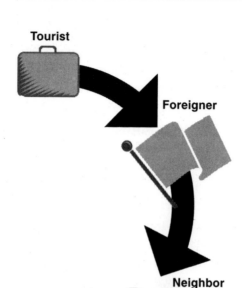

Phase Three: Neighbor
Building Relationships

People who have lost their security and significance are often very slow to build new networks. Yet developing an active network is one of the quickest ways to move through the Foreigner Phase. The most important aspect of significance is self-confidence. If people feel that they make a significant contribution to their customers, they begin to build a new sense of security and significance.

Building a network is not only essential in building a sense of security and significance, but it is imperative for accomplishing a mission. By asking yourself the following questions, you can begin to evaluate your network:

1. Who do I go to for advice?
2. Who do I go to for fun?
3. Who do I go to for affirmation and support?
4. Who do I go to for challenge?
5. Who do I go to for inspiration?
6. Who do I go to for mentoring?

Evaluate the six or more names on the list. The names should be people who stretch you, encourage you, entertain you, affirm you and stand by you through thick and thin. Each question should have a different person to fill in the blank.

Every person in your network is an integral part of your life, helping you to handle life's transitions. Perhaps you never all meet together. Many of these people don't even know each other. That is OK. A network is not a group of people that meet with you for support on a regular basis. A network is a group of people who meet the significant needs in your life when they arise.

I was meeting with the training director of a growing and dynamic silicon-chip manufacturing company. He had only been on the job for about six months and was having the time of his life. In his late 40's, he had felt burned out in his former job. As he was looking for a new career, he capped on his analytical and relational skills, and his strength in teaching, and chose the field of training and development. He laid out his plan by joining the local chapter of the American Society for Training and Development. That is where I first met him.

He announced at the first meeting what he had done in his previous life and his desire to join our ranks. Within six months, he had the job he wanted as the director of training and development. When I asked him how he got the job, he told me that he had developed a networking tree. He began with eleven primary contacts at the base of his networking tree and then branched it out to over 99 appointments. He made 450 phone calls to set up those 99 contacts. Out of those 99 contacts, he had five job interviews. One of those interviews turned into the job he wanted. On the job he finally got, he had eight referrals that led him to the person who hired him.

One more observation about networks should be emphasized here. Networks are dynamic. They change. Over the years I have had many people in my network. Associations offer an opportunity for developing networks. As a member of the National Speakers Association and The American Society for Training and Development, I have the potential to broaden and strengthen my network. Think of societies and associations as a fantastic resource for your network. People who join committees, volunteer for special assignments and begin to build new relationships seem to manage transitions most successfully. This is the fastest way to move from the Neighbor Phase to Phase Four.

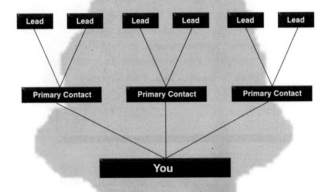

NETWORKING TREE

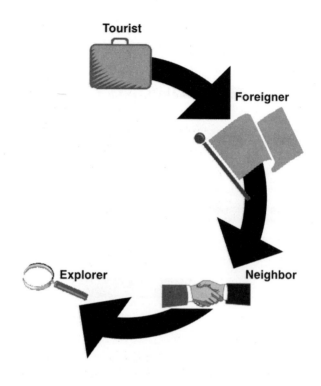

Phase Four: Explorer

Language and customs are just part of the learning curve for people moving into a new culture. The quicker people learn the language, the more they feel at home. Transitions in the work place introduce new terms and new systems. Each new transition seems to have its own software application.

Perhaps you've found in some cases that ancient Sanskrit would be easier to learn than a new software program.

The major objection many have to the Explorer Phase is that they suddenly feel unproductive and slow, when they were formerly highly productive. In their old system, they were doing their job tasks intuitively. Now their tasks have become cognitive. A cognitive task is a task that takes total concentration because we can do only one cognitive task at a time. Think of when we first learned to drive a car. Careful attention was necessary for every aspect of the process, including steering, shifting, signaling, changing lanes, parking, looking over the shoulder, and all the million and one other things we focused on. However, after we learned these basic skills and had years of driving experience, the same tasks that once occupied so much of our concentration became intuitive tasks. In contrast to cognitive tasks, many intuitive tasks can be performed at the same time. When operating intuitively, drivers can talk on the cell phone and sip their cappuccino, while shifting, signaling and changing lanes all at the same time. At this point, driving has become an intuitive task.

Transitions upset our status quo and change tasks which were formerly intuitive into cognitive ones. They do this in two ways. First, when we are given new tasks, new software, new systems, new terms and new responsibilities, we must cognitively focus on each of these tasks until they become intuitive. After we have been doing these tasks for a while, we can do many of them subconsciously and simultaneously.

But there is a second reason that the person in transition

is thrown back into cognitive task mode. When I am driving my car and talking on the phone, and all of a sudden it starts raining and hailing so that I can barely see the front of my car, I must get off the phone and put down my coffee and simply focus on driving. As I seek to maneuver my car through the changes in the road conditions, I find my heart pounding like it did when I first learned to drive. My intuitive driving task has just become cognitive again. What has made the difference? Stress. The stress of change can be the difference between what is cognitive and what is intuitive.

People who understand cognitive and intuitive tasks are aware of the time it takes to learn new systems and of the impact stress can have on those very same tasks. But before we begin attacking cognitive tasks, let us think for a moment what life would be like without them. Imagine the same scenario... I am driving in my car, drinking my cappuccino, talking on the cell phone, making a lane change while a howling storm is pelting hail against my windshield and the visibility on the road is extremely poor. I could say I'm operating in intuitive driving mode, but what do you think would be the end result of my intuitive driving? Disaster! If we didn't have the ability to think cognitively, to break tasks down into manageable increments, we would have disastrous instances all the time. Cognitive thinking allows us to process potentially dangerous situations in bite-sized pieces so that we can return to an intuitive mode once the danger is eliminated.

How do we manage this phase in the work place? Managers and supervisors must allow their work teams to learn new skills. Laughter and fun also can be a great stress buster in times of transition, particularly when we are feeling the heat of learning a new computer system, job or management system. I was working with a medical team one time and the stress was very high. The new systems that were set in place, particularly the new computer system, had thrown everyone into high stress. We were talking about how to create some more fun in the workplace while at the same time remaining sensitive to the feelings of the patients (you can't have doctors and nurses cackling in the halls when people are deathly ill).

One of the nurses suggested that the next day each person bring in a baby picture and place it on the bulletin board. I must admit that I wasn't all that excited about the idea. At first, I didn't see how it would reduce any stress. But I was wrong. At break time, I found the staff gathered all around the bulletin board laughing and trying to identify the pictures. It was a riot. Soon a contest was underway. It was amazing how this small activity had reduced the stress during a hard time.

What do you do for fun? What makes you laugh? When we learn to lighten up and enjoy life, it is amazing how our relationships, our work and our culture shock will improve, especially when we can learn to laugh at ourselves.

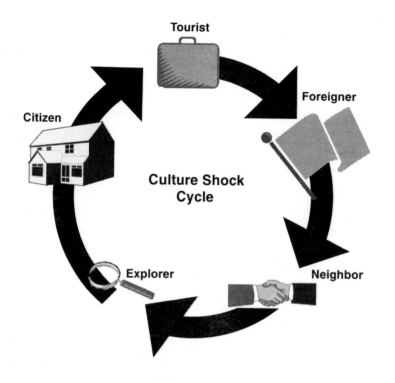

Tourist

Foreigner

Citizen

Culture Shock
Cycle

Explorer

Neighbor

Phase Five: Citizen

The last phase is the Citizen Phase. The citzen is no longer an outsider. The citizen is at home. However, the citizen phase can become another crisis stage. Citizens can become so entrenched in a culture that they find themselves complacent and in a rut. Similarly, workers in the Citizen Phase may become comfortable and resistant to change. When this happens, growth comes to a screeching halt. It is during this stage that we can lose our passion for change and growth. I was facilitating a workshop one time when a lady asked me this question: "Tom, are you going to talk about trying to keep everything the same? I like my life just as it is and I am so afraid that something is going to change. I don't want anything to change." As she was talking, I saw some people nodding their heads in agreement.

As I addressed this woman's question, my hope was that she would learn to quit resisting change. She was a comfortable citizen and wanted to remain a tourist all of her life. The logical extension of her thinking is what we call "cacooning." In fear, we try to build boxes around ourselves to protect us from an unknown future.

Culture Shock: Get Used to It!

You guessed it. The five phases of culture shock are essential to master because for the rest of our lives, we will be experiencing varying degrees of culture shock. Just when we finally settle into the Citizen Phase and nestle into a new comfort zone, another change strikes and we are thrust into the Tourist Phase all over again. Whether we're dealing on a personal or professional level, change is inevitable, and we must learn to move through it successfully. If we get stuck at any phase for too long, we risk survival mode living. Like a wheel that must keep spinning in order to gain ground, we must keep in motion through the cyclical phases of culture shock. When we hit Citizen Phase, we must begin to anticipate the next tour. By maintaining our intellectual capital, we should be able to anticipate some of these changes. The introduction of new software, new policies and procedures, new societal structure, new industry operation standards, and even new family members, all are evidences of change that create a need for us to grow and adapt as well. Experiencing new and constantly newer culture is a wonderful thing. Learning to diminish the shock is the goal of our journey.

Essential Four: Leverage Your Value With Intellectual Capital

> *Wise people learn when they can.*
> *Fools learn when they must.*
> ◆ Duke of Wellington
> *It's not what we don't know*
> *that gives us trouble,*
> *It's what we know that ain't so.*
> ◆ Will Rogers

One major problem with interpreting a new piece of music is our tendency to keep hearing John Philip Sousa. How can we look to the future? How can we get a feel for a new beat that is different from the beats we've grown used to? Interpretation of a changing score is the most exciting aspect of facing change. What does it mean to interpret our future? Must we be clairvoyant? Think of the conductor who leads an orchestra. What does it take for the conductor to interpret the sheet music? It takes knowledge, the ability to read music, to know how 4/4 differs from 3/4, how staccato differs from legato. In general, a conductor must know how to conduct! Musicians who know how to interpret all of those tiny black dots and lines on a new piece of music love to pick up a new score. Great conductors can feel the rhythm and make sense of the cacophony of musical instruments. They often pore over hundreds of musical scores before they pick the few that they are going to introduce to the orchestra.

Just as the bandleader has to interpret all of the parts of a score, we must be able to interpret the options and opportunities set before us. As we interpret each of these alternatives correctly, we can make better decisions about our future.

> ♦ The person who knows not, and knows not that he knows not, is a fool – shun him.
>
> ♦ The person who knows not, and knows that he knows not, is a child – teach him.
>
> ♦ The person who knows, and knows not that he knows, is asleep – wake him.
>
> ♦ And the person who knows, and knows that he knows, is a leader – follow him.
>
> ♦ Persian Proverb

Every time I hear the above ancient proverb, I can't help but thinking how relevant it is today. How do you find someone who knows and knows that he knows in a society where knowledge is changing so rapidly? I recently attended the medical school graduation of a family friend. The doctor who was speaking told the graduates that they had merely learned how to learn, because medical information was changing by more than 10% each year. If they didn't keep up, they would be out of date in a few years. Like these young graduating doctors, we must make an investment in our futures. It is impossible to have success on a continuing basis if we don't devote time, energy and other resources to gaining knowledge, wisdom and experience. It is not enough to simply attend a conference, college or an eight-hour job. We must go beyond our own industry and have an understanding of the world around us in order to size up change as it occurs and remain on the cutting edge. We must endeavor to gain greater insight into our immediate surroundings, our communities, our industries and ultimately our world.

I was in my early thirties when I decided to tackle graduate school. I wanted to become a leader and realized that my philosophy of not letting books interfere with my undergraduate education had caught up with me. My goal was to spend three years in the library, find the answers I was searching for and walk away equipped as a powerful leader. Within weeks of my first quarter, I was swamped with information and felt completely overwhelmed. After finals week, I trudged into a professor's office listless and discouraged. Half an hour later, I walked out, having learned another important life lesson.

My professor told me that there is no such thing as an instantaneous leader. A leader knows that he knows, not because he has some piece of information, but because he has mastered a system of learning, of collecting data, interpreting it and applying it in life. I discovered that the most significant part of my education was learning to interpret the knowledge around me. Interpretation is wisdom, and wisdom is very different than mere knowledge.

Jan Nestler, founder and Executive Director of The Eastside Adult Day Service was working at a dead-end job with no challenge. She needed a change. She had an idea, but didn't have the slightest clue how to develop the growing passion in her heart. Her idea – many senior adults are in need of supportive services on a daily basis. When this idea struck Jan over 15 years ago, she could only find five other groups in the state of Washington who provided care for frail adults during the day. Jan saw a need, but didn't know how she could pull it off.

She began by asking questions. Research at the local library uncovered a manual telling how the YMCA and other organizations had developed their structure. She checked out the book. After reading the first chapter, she called together a meeting of doctors, nurses, accountants and lawyers. About 40 people came to that meeting and listened as she described her passion. She divided them into groups as the first chapter of the book described. When the meeting was over, she didn't know how to continue, so she went home and read the second chapter and called another meeting. About 30 people showed up to the second meeting. She exhausted the ideas in the second chapter and called a third meeting after reading the third chapter.

Finally, she recruited 12 board members, organizing her board like the book described, and opened up shop. She found a local church that had a couple of rooms unused during the week where they allowed her to start. She began with five adults and met there for a few months until they outgrew the two rooms and were forced to find a larger "home." Another local church allowed the new program to use their vacant manse where the services were allowed to grow for several years. But soon they outgrew those facilities. Today the Eastside Adult Day Services now provides a full range of activities by a staff of trained social workers and medical personnel for more than 100 older adults who are dropped off each day. In the evening, another 30-40 younger adults with developmental disabilities fill the Center and participate in a bunch of fun activities.

After tremendous growth and change, Jan called me in as a consultant to meet with their board. Jan had progressed from merely reading books to incorporating consultants in the process. The Eastside Adult Day Services was in the midst of expanding from their one location to two, and significant changes were being enacted with a doubling of the staff and operation at two locations.

Jan had a passion to make a difference. She took her passion and vision and focused them into a mission – to provide adult day services for seniors. She increased her intellectual capital by going to the library and learning how to organize a non-profit organization. Out of her study, networking and hard work, she developed a plan. She had many setbacks and periods of discouragement, but she never gave up her hard work. Most of all Jan never lost her passion for her vision. She believed the frail older adult community needed a comfortable, safe place to be valued and allowed to maintain a level of independence.

As I was facilitating a weekend retreat for her board members, I heard Jan tell her story of the founding of the Eastside Adult Day Services to new board members. We all caught her passion. It was contagious. When I walked into The Eastside Adult Day Services in Bellevue and watched the staff caring for older adults and adults with disabilities, their passion for what they were doing was obvious. Jan heard the music. Her board heard the music. Her staff heard the music.

My mind went back to the day I had regained my passion – the day the music began again in my life. As I sat listening to Jan spread her vision, I was filled with a new excitement as I saw my own passion impacting those around me. It was a moment of clarity in life for me when things came full circle. I could still hear the music playing and I longed with greater passion to restore hope, encouragement and perseverance to those around me so that they too could experience the pleasure and richness of a symphonic life.

A few years ago I was in the Midwest training a financial planner. I questioned John at length about his success. During his first year as a financial planner and life insurance salesman, he earned over $250,000, so I asked him the "Big Bopper" question, "What is the secret of your success?"

He paused for a moment and explained that he was selling suits at Dalton's when he decided that he needed to make a change. He started selling life insurance and determined that he would learn everything he could about life insurance and the financial planning industry. In order to do this, John determined to get up early each day and study for an hour or two before beginning his sales day. He also disciplined himself to study each night until midnight. In addition, he started meeting with a study group. Each year, the group rented a cabin and spent five days teaching each other everything they could about their industry. John's goal was to know more than anyone else did in his office. He began to feel he was accomplishing his goal when at the end of the year people were constantly coming up to him for information — and he was the new kid on the block.

I asked John if he still kept up his intense study schedule. He said that he still spent a couple hours a week in rigorous study so that he would be able to advise his clients using the latest up-to-date information. He also tried to meet ten times a year with his study group (sometimes they did not meet that goal), but they never gave up their yearly retreat to Vail, Colorado, where they spent five days together skiing and studying. Each one would write a paper and present it to the group.

A Matter of Discipline

The old saying "knowledge is power" has never been more relevant. Charles Handy, in his book, *The Age of Paradox*,[1] describes intelligence as the new form of property, the acquisition of which is the basis for the measurement of wealth. What he is saying is that there is a direct proportion between the amount of wealth and power one possesses and the ability to acquire and apply knowledge in the form of information and technology. Robert Reich, former secretary of labor, says that those people who deal with numbers and ideas, problems and words only make up about 20% of the population, and they are the ones who are getting richer, while the other 80% are getting poorer. Leaders must be both visionaries and life-long students. Successful leaders are consistently open to new ideas and new strategies for challenging old patterns. They attend conferences, network with others and eagerly seek ways to maintain their competitive edge.

You don't have to stay up until midnight every evening poring over sales journals like John did. But if you want to

---

[1] Handy, Charles, *The Age of Paradox,* Harvard Business School Press, 1995

confidently approach any new piece of music, you can practice the following guideline.

Spend an hour every day (seven hours a week) in the following exercise:

STEPS TO INCREASING INTELLECTUAL CAPITAL

♦ Read daily newspaper
   Daily: 20 minutes   Weekly: 2 hours
♦ Read monthly trade journals
   Weekly: 1 hour
♦ Research on the Internet (e.g., advantagepoint.com)
   Weekly: 1 hour
♦ Read "out of box" periodicals (e.g., *Fast Company*)
   Weekly: 1 hour
♦ Read your professional magazines/journals
   Weekly: 1 hour
♦ Read at least one non-fiction book a month
   Weekly: 1 hour

TOTAL

♦ Weekly: 7 hours

   With the above plan, you have spent an hour a day (seven hours a week) in increasing your broad knowledge. In addition, I have found other motivational and informational activities helpful in supplementing my intellectual capital.

Consider the following activities as you explore how to increase your intellectual capital:

- ♦ Listen to tapes while driving.
- ♦ Take classes from work or your local college.
- ♦ Attend workshops (at least two a year).
- ♦ Network with a core group of people in your industry on a monthly, quarterly, semiannual or annual basis to share thoughts, ideas, strategies and encouragement.

An intimate knowledge of the score is the first prerequisite for a great conductor. Intimate knowledge gives the conductor the understanding of what the composer is intending to communicate to the audience. Intimate knowledge requires diligence. Great conductors spend hours studying one score. And no conductors are endowed innately with this knowledge of music; they must arrive at it by hard work.

Reaching Beyond

One of the greatest lessons I learned occurred when I lost my job and was forced to begin again. As I went through the process of regaining a new sense of identity and purpose, I was struck by the idea that knowledge of my own industry was not enough. In fact, as I began to create my own future, I discovered that 90% of my time was spent in selling myself and 10% of my time was spent in actually doing what I do – motivational speaking, consulting, team building and writing. I was an overnight salesman without many sales skills. So I began to burn the midnight oil and read anything I could find that pertained to sales and marketing. I listened to tapes, read books, trade magazines, publications – whatever I could find. I attended conferences and seminars and listened to great salesmen and women in the field. And what I discovered was that sales and marketing are areas that dramatically influence success in nearly any business. The strategies of communication, planning, preparation, presentation and closing are elements that are a part of most companies and organizations. As I gained knowledge of sales and marketing, I made connections between concepts that I learned and elements of my own business. As I began to apply my knowledge, I found myself gaining more and more clients and ultimately discovered my own presentations were richer and more meaningful.

We live in a world where technology seems to be constantly updating itself and the time periods between new software releases are growing exponentially shorter and shorter. In view of the rapid pace of life around us, it is easy to become discouraged at times and overwhelmed. So, what is the key to remaining current in our industry and world? One important reminder: We will never know all there is to know in our industry or world. This simple statement may be enough to give you the encouragement and incentive to press on. Education is a lifelong process. Don't be discouraged that you don't know everything or that others know more than you do. If you follow the 7-hour a week guideline for any amount of time and remain consistent, you will find yourself growing in your knowledge of both your industry and the world and will maintain a competitive edge. The key is to persevere and keep reading, studying, observing and listening to the world around you.

DanceTV is an excellent example of a company that has persevered in a time of incredible change. My son and daughter-in-law were inspired three years ago to produce a video and CD on ballroom dancing. Initially, they believed the best market would be through television advertisements. But the Internet was developing as a relatively new market at that time as well. My son Thom and his wife Amy decided that they needed to increase their intellectual capital. With no prior knowledge of the Internet world, they began by learning Perl and HTML and the best graphics programs available. In addition, they began networking with other Internet marketers around the world through news groups and mailing lists. They read dozens of books and articles to keep up with the latest trends in Internet marketing and publicity. Finally, they constructed a large website filled with 200 pages worth of free information as well as a section on how to order their product. Within two months, their orders increased by 500%. Their Internet site at www.dancetv.com has become one of the Internet's largest traveled dance sites boasting over a million hits per month. Based on their incredible Internet success, they are currently in the process of producing four more ballroom dance videos. If they had not sought to increase their intellectual capital and been willing to explore a new market, they would have missed an audience that was eager to acquire their products and services.

In view of Thom and Amy's Internet success and passion for maintaining their intellectual capital in a changing world, I hired them two years ago to develop Advantage Point's online presence at www.advantagepoint.com. Five years ago, I would have thought Internet marketing wasn't necessary. Few companies had the vision then that mass marketing through an Internet medium would be the wave of the future. Today, companies that don't have websites are considered behind the times. Thom and Amy have been an inspirational addition to Advantage Point and have given me a new appreciation for maintaining intellectual capital in an age where technology is changing so rapidly around us.

Jan, John, Thom and Amy all know what it is to increase their intellectual capital. They each run very different businesses: adult day care, financial planning and on-line marketing. None of them knew anything about these fields before they started. But they all share one essential thing in common. They learned. In the words of the Persian proverb, "They know and know that they know – follow them."

Essential Five: Focus Your Dream

> *Our plans miscarry because they have no aim. When a man does not know what harbor he is making for, no wind is the right wind.*
>
> ♦ Seneca the Younger
> Roman Statesman

Linus was watching TV one day when Lucy walked into the room and changed the channel. Turning around, Linus said, "Hey what makes you think you can just walk right in here and take over?" Lucy held up her hand and wiggled her five fingers and said, "These five fingers say so. Individually, they're nothing, but when I curl them together like this into a single unit, (she made a fist and stuck it in Linus's face) they form a weapon that is terrible to behold." In the last picture, Lucy is watching her TV program while Linus stands off in the corner gazing at his fingers. Looking down at them, he asks, "Why can't you guys get organized like that?"[1]

Like Linus's fingers, we carry around bits and pieces of information which leave us feeling disjointed and anemic, when we should be pulling everything together in a powerful picture of the future. We have some knowledge, ideas, dreams

---

[1] Charles M. Schultz, *Peanuts Treasury*, Holt, Rinehart & Winston, San Francisco, 1968

and vision. But how do we take all of our knowledge, our ideas, our dreams and our vision and focus them?

Jan Scruggs had a dream. He wanted to create a memorial for the men and women of the United States armed forces who gave their lives in and remain missing from the Vietnam War. Jan knew the power of a focused vision. But building a memorial for soldiers who had fought in the Vietnam War in the 1970's did not exactly inspire public support. In spite of seemingly overwhelming odds against him, Jan was able to raise the $8 million for the Vietnam Memorial and to involve opposites such as George McGovern and Barry Goldwater. He accomplished his goal by using a word that would be accepted by both sides and bring unity. The word was *veterans*. The mission of the memorial was to begin a process of national reconciliation by shifting focus from American national policy to the veterans who served in the war. By focusing on the veterans, political view on the Vietnam War became irrelevant. The memorial stands today as a veteran's memorial, not a war memorial. The word "vet" brought focus. The word "war" would have brought conflict.[2]

Finding that One Word

How do you find that word? How do you find that focus so that your energy will be focused into accomplishing your vision? Think for a minute about these powerful words that most of us learned in grade school:

---

[2] Walt Wiley, "20 Years Later, Impact Memories of Vietnam War Not Forgotten," The Sacramento Bee, April 27, 1995

We the People of the United States, in Order to form a more perfect Union, establish Justice, insure domestic Tranquility, provide for the common defense, promote the general Welfare, and secure the Blessings of Liberty to ourselves and our Posterity, do ordain and establish this Constitution for the United States of America.

Why has this document become so revered? How has it lasted through times of incredible difficulty and change? Notice how clearly it lays out our government's purpose and mission. Thirteen independent states, loosely connected in a confederation, fragmented and bickering, found unity and direction in those words. In the same way, organizations and individuals need to clearly focus their dreams.

Twice a year I participate with Tug and Judy Miller in the National R.V. Park Institute, a week-long school for people who would like to change careers and build, own, and manage an R.V. park. The participants come from all walks of life (engineers, police officers, ranchers, secretaries, teachers), but they all have one thing in common – they want a change in their life and they are attending this school to determine if running an R.V. park would help them fulfill their passion for change. The school offers a very intense week covering all aspects of R.V. park management from electrical systems, to sewer systems, to marketing.

As part of their program, I open the week on Sunday night with a motivational session and speak again on Monday morning. The focus is on managing change and building dynamic teams that are customer-focused. We break up into four teams and each team plans an R.V. park. Of the four teams, one is a mountain park, one is a highway park, one is a city park and one is an ocean park. Each team then answers the following six questions to help them find that word of focus for their park, their work team and their marketing plan:

Who are we?
Use some adjectives to describe your park.

What do we do?
What will we do in this visionary picture of our park? What are the tasks we will do for our customers?

Who is our customer?
Who is going to benefit from our vision?

What impact do we have on our customers?
How will our customers benefit from staying at our park?

What makes our park unique?
What do we have that other parks in this field do not have?

How do we market our park?
How can we get this message out to the people who need to hear it?

Recently one of the teams answered the questions this way:

Who are we?
We are a family oriented, oceanside R.V. Park.

What do we do?
We provide year-round family activities for R.V'ers.

Who is our customer?
Our customers are families from around the world.

What impact do we have on our customers?
We provide them with safety, security, fun, oceanfront sites, family activities, large R.V. sites, and clean areas for recreation.

What makes our park unique?
We have an oceanfront location, highly trained and courteous staff, and family activities.

How do we market our park?
By providing for our guests a clean, safe, and quiet park managed by a highly trained and customer-focused staff, people will recommend our park to their friends and neighbors.

From their answers, they developed the following focused mission statement:

> The mission of the Ocean Side R.V. Park is to be recognized as *THE* place to spend a restful, stress-free, fun time on the California coast. We offer recreational, educational, and creative family activities.
>
> We will accomplish our mission by providing for our guests a clean, safe, and quiet park managed by a highly trained and customer-focused staff.

We value . . .
Guest satisfaction
Staff development
Clean facilities
Safety
Quiet and privacy
Family activities
Ethnic diversity (encouraging worldwide guests)

I have each group go through this exercise so that they can be very focused in their business plan, their marketing and their expectations for the customers that stay at their park. I also suggest that they have their work teams answer these questions each year and develop their team mission statement for the year. When teams own a focused statement, they have a credible claim to accomplish it.

What is true for the R.V. park is true for the individual

also. Our individual dreams must be focused, and the six questions can help us focus these dreams into an accomplishable
reality. Answer the following six questions about your personal vision:

Who am I?

In light of my reading, my visioning and my goals,
who do I want to be? What role do I want to
fill? (Use some adjectives to describe yourself.)

What do I do?

What will I do in this visionary picture of myself?
What are the tasks I will do?

Who is my customer?

Who is going to benefit from my vision, talent, gifts,
and services?

What impact do I have on my customers?

How will my customers benefit from my service or
product? How will they be different?

What makes me unique?

What do I have that other people in this field do not
have?

How will I market this service or product?

How can I get this message out to the people who
need to hear it?

Focus and the Non-Self-Employed

This book is not just intended for the self-employed. Perhaps the thought of starting your own company or being self-employed does not stir your passions. In fact, the thought of it totally drains any passion from you and leaves you feeling tired and a little overwhelmed. You would love to find a position in a company that you could be passionate about. Or maybe you are someone who has been left after a downsizing and you are not sure what your future looks like. The exercises in this manual are for you also. You can still gain the confidence and hope for your future by working carefully through these steps.

Answer the six questions about the position you want. Joan, a downsized computer specialist, found her focus by answering these six questions:

Who am I?
  ♦ I am a dependable and committed Internet special-ist who is the company expert.

What do I do?
  ♦ I develop software.
  ♦ I write PERL scripts.
  ♦ I develop a relational database backed website.

Who is my customer?
Internal:
  ♦ My company
  ♦ My boss

♦ My colleagues
External:
♦ Our clients

What makes me unique?
♦ I am dependable.
♦ I love to learn and keep up with changes.
♦ I have experience and education to give me a competitive advantage.
♦ I am a team player.

What impact do I have on my customers?
♦ I reduce viewer's stress by designing user-friendly websites.
♦ I increase the bottom line of our company by giving our potential and present customers value-added information.
♦ I provide greater income for our sales teams through qualified leads generated on our website.
♦ I contribute to a winning team through my dependability.

How will I market this service or product?
♦ I report my value to the company in written and verbal reports.
♦ I participate and contribute in meetings and training.
♦ I join committees to work on extra projects.

Focused Mission Statement:

I am contributing significantly to the growth and profitability of (company name) by developing interactive websites for our external and internal customers. I am the company Internet expert and consult with each department (eg, marketing, training) about how to improve service, quality, growth and profitability through the Internet. I accomplish my mission through constant personal and professional development and proactive participation above and beyond the expected.

What is the one word?

This person is a computer specialist. But in her reading and exploration, she decided that she would become the resident expert on the Internet and develop an interactive website for her company. Her one word of focus (actually two): Internet Specialist.

A Few More Hints as You Focus Your Vision

- Write the future in the present ("I am" rather than "I will be").
- Be a visionary thinker (look beyond where you are today).
- Think of how you can contribute to the growth and profitability of a company (or yourself).

- Narrow the vision to a focus that you can get passionate about.
- In your vision, find that one word that focuses your mission (or a few possible words).
- Answer the six questions in less than ten words (no paragraphs).

For information on the National RV Park Institute call: (530) 823-2316

Essential Six: Think and Plan Strategically

> *Entrepreneurs see change as the norm and as healthy. Usually they do not bring about change themselves. But—and this defines entrepreneur and entrepreneurship— the entrepreneur always searches for change, responds to it, and exploits it as opportunity.*
>
> ♦ Peter Drucker

I was meeting an employee of one of my clients for coffee to go over an assignment I had given her. When we met, she handed me a blank piece of paper. I thought she was going to tell me that she didn't have time to do the project. Her response took me by surprise. I had asked her to think strategically. She told me that she couldn't complete the assignment because she didn't know how to think. In all of her education, she had never been taught to think. She could memorize facts and get excellent grades, but when she was asked to think, she could only stare at a blank piece of paper. I had asked her to think strategically. In actuality, Suzanne knew how to think. But she did not know how to think strategically. For the next hour we talked about how to think strategically, and by the end of the session, she had thought of some things to write down on her paper.

What Suzanne learned that morning is something that we all must understand if we are going to become strategic thinkers. You don't need an MBA to think strategically. In fact, you don't need a BA to think strategically. Strategic thinking can be achieved by following several logical steps which build upon a focused vision.

The Four Steps to Thinking Strategically

1. Set a focused vision – where you want to be
2. Identify the impact factors
3. Fill the gap with major steps
4. Determine the baby steps

Step One: Set A Focused Vision

The process of thinking strategically begins with two essentials that we've already discussed. As you entertain visions of hope and success and begin to focus those dreams and ideas into a concise mission or goal, you will enter into strategic thinking territory. Your focused vision statement is stated in the present; however, it will actually occur in the future so you'll need to plan the strategic steps to reach that vision.

Step Two: Identify the Impact Factors

As you look at your focused mission statement, start by taking five minutes to write down one-word descriptions of all the factors that could have an effect on your vision. Come up with as many words as you can. You probably will list 30-40 words. Some words that may appear on your list include:

- ♦ Money
- ♦ Economy
- ♦ Family
- ♦ Health
- ♦ Loans
- ♦ Education
- ♦ Time

This is a brainstorming exercise to help you explore possible positive and negative factors that will have an impact on your success. As you stretch your mind, you will be prepared to tackle Step Three.

Step Three: Identify the Major Steps

Strategic planners call these steps the Critical Success Factors or CSF's. These are the factors that are critical to the success of your vision. The Critical Success Factors will follow these rules:

♦ Each CSF must be necessary.
♦ Begin each CSF with "I must."
♦ Altogether, the CSF's must be sufficient to accomplish
   your vision.
♦ CSF's are statements of hope (goals), not how.
♦ Each CSF focuses on one thing.
♦ There should be at least four and no more than eight
CSF's (more then eight becomes too overwhelming).

Some of your Critical Success Factors might be:

♦ I must get my degree.
♦ I must earn $50,000.
♦ I must develop an aggressive marketing program.
♦ I must write a book (or articles).
♦ I must develop my network.

The Critical Success Factors are the short-term goals that identify the six to eight steps to accomplishing your focused mission.

Step Four: Identify the Baby Steps - Thinking Tactically

The fourth step to filling in the gap is to think tactically –
or along the lines of baby steps. Here's where the *how* comes
in. You know what you want to do, but how are you going to
accomplish your Critical Success Factors? It is time to think

tactically.

In the movie *What About Bob?* Bob (Bill Murray) is a troubled individual who seeks counseling/psychotherapy from Richard Dreyfuss, who in the film has recently authored the best-seller <u>Baby Steps</u>. As Bob begins to take "baby steps," he discovers that his enormous problems can be broken down into manageable pieces that he can tackle individually. If you haven't seen the film, it will provide some comic relief and perhaps a little perspective on the idea of taking baby steps. You may even discover that your problems aren't as big as you thought they were. Strategic thinking involves breaking down our major goals into manageable baby steps like Bob did. Just picture yourself saying "Baby steps into the elevator... Baby steps onto the sidewalk... Baby steps to the cab... Baby steps to the apartment building..."

I was having lunch with a client a few weeks ago when she told me that she would only be with the company for three more years. She and her husband had bought property in the Cayman Islands and were in the process of building a home there. She told me that her husband was going to design websites, teach Tae Kwon Do and scuba dive, and she was going to write. At that time, they were in the fifth year of a seven-year plan.

She outlined how they had bought the property and were looking at building plans. They plan on spending the first year working together building their home. She told me that people kept laughing at them and telling them they would never make it on that little island. But they visit every year, are getting to know their neighbors and are saving every penny so they can take an early retirement and enjoy a life in paradise. They are accomplishing their goals because they learned how to turn their vision into a tactical program.

Strategic thinking is big picture. It is the "what" and focuses on the future. Tactical thinking is small picture. It focuses on the tasks, systems and business processes that you need to do to accomplish your Critical Success Factors. Strategic planning purists will argue that some business processes are strategic and some are tactical. They will define strategic as long range and tactical as short range. However, for over 20 years, I have used a system which combines strategic and tactical steps into an overall plan for people and organizations. I have found that combining them creates simplicity which has been the reason for our success.

Defining our baby steps is not that difficult. We take each of our Critical Success Factors and develop the action steps necessary to accomplish them. For each CSF, we develop a business process that must meet the following guidelines:

- Each process must follow a "verb +" structure.
- Each process must be necessary.
- Together all processes must be sufficient to accomplish the CSF.
- Each process must be measured by a date (when it will be done).

Sample business processes to accomplish our CSF's might include the following:

- Submit application to the University by January 13th.
- Attend weekly meetings with a networking group.

+ Join our local association by January 30th.
+ Get involved in a local association committee for networking by February 1st.
+ Make 25 phone calls a day.
+ Spend one hour a week doing research.

After you have done this for each CSF, establish a time line. List each business process for each month. This is the key to accomplish your vision. Without these tactical steps, your vision is only a dream. Each business process needs to be broken down into daily tasks. As you work on your daily tasks, you can accomplish your focused mission.

Two of the best examples of strategic thinkers that I know are Mike and Linda Jones, owners of Rhapsody International, Inc. Rhapsody is a multimillion-dollar company located in Northern California, specializing in the design and manufacture of gift items such as gift bags, cards, wrapping paper, photo frames, bookmarks and notebooks. Mike and Linda believe that their success as a company is based on their commitment to God as well as to their employees, customers and vendors. While they have experienced successes and failures in business, they have learned from past mistakes and bad partnerships, and as entrepreneurs, have pressed on and learned what it takes to make it in the business world. One of the most important steps they have taken is to ensure a firm foundation of trust among their employees, their customers and their vendors. Reputation is key at Rhapsody. Mike and Linda believe that if Rhapsody cannot be relied upon to produce quality merchandise in a timely manner with little-to-no errors along the way, the success of the company will be fleeting. But Mike and Linda admit that the reputation of Rhapsody has been difficult to maintain, especially during times of incredible change and transition…but not impossible.

In their startup days, maintaining an error-free (or near error-free) margin at Rhapsody was easy. Mike and Linda were responsible for absolutely everything. But as the company experienced growing pains and was forced to expand and acquire employees, a new system was needed to keep the high standards and quality service that Rhapsody customers and vendors had grown accustomed to. According to Linda, this was the toughest transition time Rhapsody had ever faced. Their employees didn't initially share Mike and Linda's vision for a dependable, error-free company. Consequently, the initial days of Rhapsody's expansion included many mistakes which were usually the result of communication problems between departments who knew little about the other departments in the company. Mike and Linda quickly realized that mistakes were detrimental not only to the reputation of the company, but to Rhapsody's bottom line. For every mistake, there was a specific cost associated with it. And while some mistakes cost more than others, they all were eating into Rhapsody's profits.

As strategic thinkers, Mike and Linda set out to solve the problem which was becoming increasingly costly and threatening their reputation with customers and vendors. They began by identifying the specific dollar amount associated with each error. Then they calculated the percentage of profit loss due to error, and set an acceptable margin of error at one-half that number. They figured that this would be an affordable rate of loss. At this point, they still needed to consider how to maintain their reputation for quality and reliability service. They came up with the following plan.

Mike and Linda gathered their employees together and told them that they would be given the percentage deemed an "acceptable margin of error" if no mistakes were made. The money would be divided up every year in December based on the number of hours each employee worked. In addition, an added incentive was given. The percentage was calculated from gross sales, so each employee was also motivated to do whatever they could to increase Rhapsody's gross. Because this percentage calculated out to a very significant bonus every December, a system of checks and balances developed at Rhapsody out of employee motivation. This decision didn't cost Mike and Linda any more money, because they would have paid the same amount (or more) just from errors. Mike told me that it is an incredible feeling to give a hard working and dedicated employee a $3500 dollar Christmas bonus. It's good for the employee and builds internal trust. But most importantly, Mike and Linda developed a synergistic team of employees with high company morale and allegiance, who were restoring Rhapsody's reputation and improving the bottom line. Through Mike and Linda's strategic thinking and commitment to God, their employees, customers and vendors, they have established a company which is ready for any of the changes that the future might bring.

Essential Seven: Keep the Faith

> *Worry is a thin stream of fear trickling through the mind.*
> *If encouraged, it cuts a channel into which all other thoughts are drained.*
>
> ♦   Arthur Somers Roche

Nighttime is one of the worst times to be thinking about changes. Sleeping and change don't mix. Try it and you'll find yourself swirling in a sea of cloudy thoughts, fear, anxiety and sleepless nights. And doubt seems darkest at night. What we need is the faith that will not only allow us to sleep, but also help us to accomplish our visions.

But what is faith? When I think of faith, I am reminded of the two nuns who ran out of gas along the roadside. They were both nurses and had a bedpan in the trunk of their car. So they decided to walk to a gas station and fill the bedpan with gas. Upon their return, as the nuns were filling their car with the gas from the bedpan, two guys drove by in a truck. Seeing what the nuns were doing, one truck driver said to the other, "Now that's what I call faith!"

The truck drivers had missed some very important information. They lacked knowledge of what was actually in the bedpan. And this is what is so often wrong with faith – there is no objective truth at the basis of faith's assumptions. Faith is no stronger than the truth of its assumptions. It is no stronger than its object. If the object is false, then the faith is false.

Faith must have an object. Just because we believe, it doesn't mean that we will accomplish our goals. At three-o-clock in the morning, when I can't sleep because of worry and doubt, I get up and look at the assumptions (knowledge) and the goals I have made. I ask myself if my assumptions are correct and if my goals are realistic. About 99% of the time I find that they are. However, I often discover that I have not dedicated myself to the steps that I said I would do in order to make these changes work.

When I started my consulting business, I discovered that I would have to spend about 90% of my time marketing the business and about 10% of my time doing what I loved. When I got several contracts, I stopped marketing. But, in a few months when all of my contracts were completed, I did not have any new business. Many self-employed individuals and people in sales jobs discover this same reality. My doubt and discouragement did not arise from a lack of business, nor did it stem from personal incompetence. Rather, it was because I had failed to follow through in some very basic commitments of marketing my business and myself.

I love the story of Odysseus from Greek mythology. Odysseus was sailing with his crew on a series of dangerous adventures. One adventure took them past the island inhabited by the Sirens. These creatures had the bodies of birds, the heads of women and voices that were so enticing that sailors were rendered powerless. When the Sirens began to sing, passing sailors were so entranced that they rushed toward the island to encounter these lovely creatures, only to be dashed upon the rocks by the treacherous surf. From this story is derived the expression, "the Siren voice of pleasure." The hunger for pleasure is often so great that perils are ignored, and in the attempt to reach our desire, we find ourselves ship-wrecked and dashed on the rocks.

Now Odysseus didn't know how he was going to successfully evade the Sirens. As he brainstormed, he arrived at two ways in which it could be done. The first was by way of equipment. Odysseus plugged up all the sailors' ears and had them lash him to a mast so he couldn't move.

But somebody came up with a better idea. A man named Orpheus worked on a ship. He was the greatest harp player in the land. The music that Orpheus made was even more beautiful than the singing of the Sirens. When the men listened to the music of Orpheus, the songs of the Sirens did not tempt them.

Odysseus' problem parallels those that are encountered during times of change. We must continually ask ourselves which song we are going to listen to. We need a faith that is grounded in truth to keep us focused and not distracted. We can lose our passion for our vision if we begin to listen to a different song. It may be a song of discouragement, or it may be a song enticing us to look in greener pastures. But whatever the song, we must determine its nature and whether or not we will choose to listen to it.

When I started Advantage Point, I had to set up some

systems to make sure that no matter how busy I became, I always devoted significant time to marketing. I had become distracted by the work I love, and had forgotten the essential activity that had gotten me the business in the first place. As the business grew, I was able to hire staff to handle this part of the job, but in the early years, I had to balance it all myself.

My minister tells me that I need to be in church every Sunday so that I can reaffirm my faith. Why does he say that? He knows that when I neglect the weekly worship, I get distracted and forget the foundation of my faith and the community of friends around me (one of my important networks). The same is true when we face any new piece of music in life.

The Object of Our Faith: Our Values

Values frame our decisions and how we see the future; however, we sometimes change these values according to the pressures of the moment. This can lead to a rickety foundation for our faith. In order to have a solid faith, we must first determine which values are constant and which are subject to change.

Values are the yardsticks by which we interpret future decisions. However, we live in a society where some yardsticks seem to be changing. We must ask ourselves two critical questions, "What are the absolutes of my value system?" and "What are the values that are constantly changing and emerging?" Sometimes the word *value* is used as a relative term. A co-ed wrote to her parents the following letter:

Dear Mom and Dad,

I just thought that I would drop you a note to let you know my changing plans. I have fallen in love with a wonderful guy named Jerry. I'm bringing him home with me for Thanksgiving so you can meet him.

He is 45 years old and has three children from his first marriage, two from his second, and one from his third. He has really had a hard time in life and has spent several years in prison, but has really been changed and I would like you to love him because I love him.

At any rate, I dropped out of school last week, although I hope to finish someday.

On the next page, the letter continued:

Mom and Dad, I just want you to know that nothing I said on the previous page is true. However, it is true that I got a "C" in math and just flunked my first English A test. And it is true that I've run out of money.

This young college freshman had learned an important lesson. Even bad news can sound good when contrasted with a poorer alternative. It's a matter of perspective. Success and failure are relative terms and their meaning depends on the yardstick we use to measure them.

I have often felt like the CEO who called his chief engineer, his vice president of marketing and his accountant into his office. He posed the same question to each one: "What is 1 + 1?" To this, the chief engineer answered, "1 + 1 is 2, plus or minus the square root of the difference between the mean and the median." The CEO knew he had the right person for the job. The vice president of marketing answered, "1 + 1 is 4 today, but if you give me until tomorrow, I bet I can make it 5." And the accountant said, "1 + 1? What do you want it to be?"

As the new millennium is on us, it is hard to know what is absolute and what is not. Like the college co-ed, we can try to adjust the bar of expectations by comparison. Her academic grades did not seem so bad when compared with a dangerous relationship. Or like the engineer, sales manager and accountant, we can interpret the same equation in different ways to satisfy our boss. Establishing values can be a frustrating process, but it is a critical element to building a sturdy interpretation window. So what do we use as our yardstick? What do we call truth?

Establishing, reaffirming and emphasizing core values are essential in times of transition. Transition can bring insecurity and a common value system bolsters security and a foundation for faith. When an orchestra looks at a new piece of music, some things are the same. Notes are notes. Key signatures are key signatures. Measures are measures. The difference each time is the arrangement of those notes and how each instrument interacts with the notes and each other. The interpretation of the new piece of music begins with a basic knowledge of what each note stands for and how they are orchestrated. Without a basic understanding – without a common yardstick – the orchestra is in total disarray.

I am reminded of the student who walked into her music professor's studio and asked him, "What do you know for sure?" Taking his tuning fork, the music teacher struck it against his knee and said, "This is A. It was A yesterday, and it will be A tomorrow. The soprano next door is singing flat. The piano in this room is flat. But this is A." What is A? What are the "A's" that we are going to base our lives on? What are the foundations of our beliefs? In order for a cause to be believable, it must be well founded and supported.

Great leaders have always established a common set of values. Moses, when he came down from the mountain, carried the Ten Commandments. The Israelites had been enslaved in Egypt, had wandered about in the desert, and were in great need of direction. The Ten Commandments established a moral code and value system that governed their relationship with God and each other. Different cultures operate under different sets of values. These values form the guiding principles by which members of such societies make decisions.

Because we live in a global society, our neighbors and colleagues often possess different value systems than we do. Identifying and clarifying our values is essential, and the process is one that we must be confident and competent in administering. With change surrounding us on all sides, it is essential to revisit, rework and recommit to our values every year. While some values never change such as integrity, honesty and a commitment to excellence, others need to be considered frequently as business, society and markets change around us.

Constant Values: Establishing a Common Yardstick

While our world is not all black and white and many things are relative, certain truths do exist which remain constant throughout time. These truths are the same today as they were yesterday, or even 3000 years ago. What are the truths that form the basis of our knowledge as we continually learn new data?

Think of what it would be like if we lived in a society where nobody obeyed the traffic laws. Green could mean go, stop or anything in between. Relative morality could be pretty dangerous in such a situation. Even if we profess a belief in a relative world, we'd probably be the first ones to file a lawsuit against an uninsured motorist who broadsided us as a result of running a red light. If we didn't have a common yardstick – a general understanding of what the traffic laws were – it would be difficult to synergistically function on our roads and highways.

Through our personal convictions, we develop value statements that must be clarified through open communication in order to secure a common yardstick. As we rely on our values to measure the success or failure of our actions and relationships, a basic understanding will be established at the team level which can provide unity during times of transition. With feelings of insecurity, uncertainty and fear swirling around the team, it is essential to establish a firm truth-based foundation by articulating the core values. When we operate under well-defined values, team security will be bolstered.

Marian Wade, the visionary who developed Service-Master, is a prime example of a person who built the success of a company around a set of four value statements. Wade was a deeply religious man whose goal in life was to serve God and people. His values have evolved over the years, but they basically are captured in the four statements that are engraved in the marble slab in the headquarters of Service Master in Downers Grove, Illinois.

1. To honor God in all we do
2. To help people develop
3. To pursue excellence
4. To grow profitably

C. William Pollard answers the question some might have about a value system that emphasizes God and profit. He says, "Profit is a means in God's world to be used and invested, not an end to be worshipped. Profit is a legitimate measurement of the value of our effort." [1]

Evolving Values

Not all values are immutable. In business, we value integrity, honesty, virtue and loyalty as moral and ethical standards. These things never change. Although we have all been "ripped off" by people who obviously do not practice these values, most of us acknowledge them as important elements in a functioning society. But some values need to be revisited, evaluated and interpreted in light of changing markets.

---

[1] *C. William Pollard, The Soul of the Firm, (New York: Harper Business, 1996) p. 20*

One of the most dramatic changes in recent years has been the changing value of foreign products. Consider Japan. In the early sixties, I worked my way through college detailing new cars. The cars were delivered from Detroit and were often a mess. I remember a rattle that we couldn't get out of a new car. I finally took the side panel completely off and discovered a coke bottle lodged inside. Even though our American cars arrived in such condition, we would make jokes about foreign imports. When the dealership I worked for started selling some foreign cars, those of us who worked in the shop detested them.

In the 1960's, "Made in Japan" usually brought to my mind images such as poor quality, junk, toys, and cheap. But today when we say, "Made in Japan," we think of quality, high tech, and expensive products that will last and last and last. What was it that changed the stereotype in the minds of most Americans? It was the consistent high quality of Japanese parts and automobiles. When it caught on that Japanese cars had quality far superior to American automobiles, a value shift occurred. What made the difference? Quality competition did. Americans woke up and had to change their value system. I am sure that American car manufacturers would have said that they believed in quality; however, it wasn't until competition forced them to change that they actually walked their talk.

Values Clarification

Sometimes people think they are committed to certain core values, when in actuality, they are espousing some lofty ideals. When put to the test, the ideals are quickly discarded. A person looking for a new car may have an underlying belief which values American cars over foreign automobiles. He limits his decision by a decision door that is framed by the American car value. Consequently, he won't even consider a foreign car. But suddenly, a rich uncle dies and the estate is selling a brand new Lexus LS 400. The same person gets first choice and can have this car if he pays the licensing fees and insurance. What does he do? He quickly changes his values and accepts the Japanese car. How easily values can shift when presented with a flashy alternative!

We must continue to test and re-test our values. The following questions must be asked regularly (either personally or corporately):

- What do I value?
- How do my values shape my decisions?
- How do my values shape my choices?
- How do my values shape my budgeting?
- How do my values shape my priorities?
- Are my values best serving my customers?
- Are my values causing me to be hypocritical?
- Are my values producing cynicism among my significant relationships?

These are just some of the questions that we as leaders need to be asking as we seek to manage change. An interpretation of our future is framed by a value system that has the following characteristics:

- Values which form a common, never-changing yardstick
- Values which evolve
- Values which are clarified through the test of decisions and actions

Getting Back to Sleep at 3 a.m.

So how do we affirm our faith and go back to sleep at 3:00 a.m.? The following steps form the object of our faith.

Steps to Keeping the Faith:

- Reaffirm your values.
- Reaffirm your vision.
- Reaffirm your focused mission (find your one word).
- Evaluate your CSF (critical success factors). Do you need to modify and change them?
- Evaluate your tactical steps. Do you need to reschedule them?

Essential Eight: Just Do It
Six Fundamentals

> *Everything must degenerate into work if anything is to happen.*
>
> ♦   Peter Drucker

When it all boils down to it, all of our great vision, focus, communication and plans comes down to one thing – work. What happens when we all show up to work on Monday morning? We begin the process of creating vision and focus through communication and planning. Most changes take place in the trenches at work, which is why the seventh essential is the most often overlooked and dynamic element. People want to be as successful as James Cameron or Andy Grove, but they want it to happen overnight. They forget that inspiration plus perspiration equals success.

Fundamental 1: Prioritize Your Day

One hot July afternoon, I was facilitating a workshop on the Florida Gulf Coast for a group of managers. Most of the group had been out fishing in the morning and I was to begin my four-hour workshop after lunch. When the group walked off of the boat, three things were obvious to me. One – they had gotten too much sun. Two – they hadn't caught enough fish. And three - they had consumed way too much beer. The group was hardly in the mood for a workshop. Most of them would have loved to find a bed and crash for a few hours. But that was not an option by senior management. They had paid the bills for their managers to spend several days together at a fishing lodge, and some motivational training classes had been thrown in. I was conducting one of the training classes, and I had been flown in that morning and was leaving that evening. I had four hours to "do my thing."

I was in a Catch-22. Changing the schedule was not an option. But this group didn't seem that interested in participating in a four-hour workshop either. I was reminded of an article I had read on the plane in which a seminar leader had conducted the following experiment. I decided to try it, and in a few minutes those managers were involved and responding fantastically.

I went to the kitchen and got a quart-sized jar. I put several large rocks in the jar and asked the question, "Is the jar full?" The managers started kidding with me and said that they were sure I could get some more rocks in the jar. Then I filled the jar with sand and asked them again, "Is the jar full?" They said that the jar looked full, but they believed there was something else I could get in the jar. They were right. I then filled the jar with water and then I changed the question. I asked them, "What is the lesson of the jar?"

Some of them said that the jar looked like their day. Their managers would keep loading more and more into their work-day. One said that the jar looked like his life – he kept adding things into his workday and his life was a mess. Although all of these could have been lessons of the jar, the lesson I built my workshop on was the following: If I hadn't put the rocks in the jar first, I would not have gotten them in the jar at all.

It's a powerful lesson. The rocks represent the highest priorities in our lives, but we often forget to put them in first, and instead fill our days with secondary essentials (and often nonessentials) like sand and water. Determining what the rocks are is the most important element in accomplishing our goals and dreams.

What are the major rocks that need to be in your day? Only you can answer this question. The primary activities (rocks) of your day are determined by your goals (CSF's). Your goals are framed by your values. Your daily activities (tactical steps/baby steps) will enable you to accomplish your goals. They will help you achieve synergistic living. Synergistic living is achieved when your total body, soul and spirit are in harmony. And maximum productivity is achieved when synergy is realized. When this happens, you can take charge of your life. And this is leadership in its most effective expression.

Fundamental 2: Take Baby Steps

We return again to the film, *What About Bob?* So, what about him? He was able to identify the baby steps in his life so that he could successfully overcome fears in his path. The world became filled with identifiable obstacles that he could tackle in small, incremental baby steps.

And think back again to Michael Jordan who broke a 32-point game into increments of 8 points per quarter. The goal of accomplishing 32 points per game may have seemed monumental, but when broken into manageable pieces (at least for Jordan), it was an accomplishable goal.

One practical tool I learned came from a successful sales executive who held to the rule of the magnificent seven. In the rapid pace of our society, it is easy to feel like there is more to do when the day is done. The job of learning to face a new piece of music is never done. Consequently, we find ourselves laying awake at night contemplating all the things we could have done or could be doing to have a more productive day. The rule of the magnificent seven helps us to sleep at night and also helps to ensure that we are accomplishing our goals. Here's the rule: Each night, before you leave your desk, write down seven tasks that you want to accomplish the next day. Some days it will be nine and others it might only be five, but on an average it will be seven. Seek to finish those tasks. When you leave your desk, you can think, "I have done today what I needed to do in order to reach my goals." If you follow the rule of the rocks and the rule of baby steps by determining and writing down seven prioritized action steps, little by little you can accomplish your goals.

Fundamental 3: Start Today - Don't Wait Until You're Perfect

Some of the best advice I ever received came from my real estate agent when we were selling our home. Kathy said to me, "Tom, don't wait until your home is perfect to sell.

You will never put it on the market. Let me look at it. I'll give you a few suggestions and let's get it on the market."

Kathy's advice is applicable to our lives also. In this life we will never be perfect. If we wait until we are perfect, we'll never be able to put ourselves on the market. We will become stagnant, waiting for perfection to be achieved, only to discover that perfection is a lot farther off than we originally thought it was. While I constantly strive to reach perfection, I am far from it. It's a lifelong pursuit.

In 1982, the book *In Search of Excellence* caused a revolution in business circles. The book focused on eight attributes that are essential for excellence in a company. The first of the book's attributes was "a bias for action." A bias for action means, *get going*. As Will Rogers said, "Even if you're sitting on the right track, if you are sitting, you are going to get run over by a fast moving train." Woody Allen put it this way, "90% of success is merely showing up." When you lay out your baby steps, it's time to get going!

Fundamental 4: Overcome Obstacles

Some years ago, when the Pope visited California, I watched a young man without arms play the guitar for him using only his feet. I had never seen anything like it before. An immigrant from Nicaragua, Tony Melendez had a lifelong dream of becoming a priest. But, after years of study, he was rejected from the priesthood when the Vatican ruled him ineligible for service. Tony returned from his rejection to Los Angeles where he taught himself to play the guitar with his feet. He supported himself sitting on the sidewalk, playing hymns for bystanders. It was there that he was discovered and invited to play and sing for the Pope. The day that Tony played his guitar for the Pope stands as an incredible affirmation of his ability to face unbelievable obstacles.

In his book, *A Gift of Hope*, Tony talks about his experience playing for the Pope:

> *After the concert I walked backstage through the waiting crowd of old friends and new... At the back of the crowd I saw a badly deformed young woman in a wheelchair. Her arms and legs were twisted, but she smiled and tried to wave as I passed. I kept walking toward the exit; then I stopped, turned around and walked back in her direction. When she saw me standing beside her, her eyes filled with tears. She reached her hand out toward me and struggled to speak. 'Tony,' she said, 'because of you, we all have hope.'*[1]

Hope is an amazing thing. It gives us the strength and courage to persevere despite unbelievable odds and obstacles. It is durable, tenacious and inspiring. But more than anything, hope is contagious. Hope reaches out to the crippled woman, and gives her hope to persevere and pass hope on to others. It keeps going and going. But, in order to have this kind of hope in the face of obstacles, we must have an in-your-face attitude toward discouragement and rejection.

---

[1] Tony Melendez, *Gift of Hope*, Angelus Media, September, 1997

Fundamental 5: Persevere with an In-Your-Face Attitude toward Discouragement and Rejection

Discouragement and rejection are elements that all successful people must deal with. George Bernard Shaw had his first five novels rejected. Monet was painting great pictures at the age of 86. Composer Richard Wagner considered the first thirty years of his life a failure. His first, second, and third operas were flops. Tennyson wrote *Crossing the Bar* when he was 83. These famous individuals shed new light on the phrase, "If at first you don't succeed, try, try again." Perseverance is key.

Tom Hanks, a former student at California State University Sacramento, is a local celebrity and inspiration for many Sacramento theatre arts students. Recently I was facilitating a faculty retreat with the Theater Arts Department at the University where Tom Hanks used to study and perform. Faculty members were talking about students who have become so involved in "acting" that they refuse to degrade themselves with lowlier positions like painting sets and working the lights. "We are actors," they respond when instructors attempt to recruit volunteers to help with set design and construction. One professor loves to tell the students how Tom Hanks painted sets, ran the lights and worked in costumes when he was a student. He was willing to do anything that would better the production, from acting to lighting.

I recently saw Tom interviewed on our local TV station. He was reminded how in his early years he had been rejected. Tom talked about how it was common for him to get 30 rejections before he ever received a part. The interviewer asked him how he dealt with such rejection. Tom said that he would get down for about 30 seconds or so and then he was ready to try out for the next part.

While I am fairly optimistic, my depression over rejection often lasts more than 30 seconds. But what I have learned is that I have to get over those feelings of rejection quickly. As I have practiced over the years, I have learned to bring down the feelings of rejection from a day to an hour. And I'm working on the Tom Hanks attitude of 30 seconds. How do we deal with rejection quickly and optimistically? One way is to immediately start working on the next project and to visualize what it can be. Our answers will always be found in the future, not in the past. If we continue to dwell on past failures, or overemphasize past successes, we can get lost in a memory cloud and make little to no progress in the future.

Fundamental 6: Never Give Up

You can have passion, knowledge, hope, focus, strategy and faith, but as the Bible says, "Faith without action is dead." All success stories I know are expressed in the discipline of hard work. When we moved to Denver in the early 70's so that I could attend graduate school, Susie was excited to get back into her teaching field. She had taken a break from teaching for five years while our boys were preschool age. Our oldest son was going into kindergarten and we decided that I would be the house dad while I attended graduate school and Susie would teach high school English – a great plan except for one thing… We found out that there were 10,000 teachers who did not have jobs in Denver.

Susie had graduated from a university in California and had a California credential. But that did not stop her. She got her Colorado credential and for one year before we moved, she wrote letters, visited and called key people in the school districts. When we moved, she did not have a job, but she kept trying. Many of the other wives of graduate students had given up on finding teaching jobs and were working in offices as secretaries. Susie kept telling me, "I'm not a secretary – I'm an English teacher. Teaching is my passion." The one person that she had connected with some months before had retired and she felt as if her only positive contact was gone. When school started, Susie substitute taught for a while and looked for jobs in the afternoons and on her days off. In the third week of school, she got a call from a high school in Jefferson County saying that they had miscalculated and needed another English teacher. The person who had retired had left instructions that if they needed to hire an English teacher, Susie should be put at the top of the list. She had that job for three years while I was in graduate school. Susie never gave up her passion, hope, strategy and faith. But it was her initiative and perseverance that reaped the fruit.

Arlene Blum is a mountaineer and leadership guru. In *Fast Company* she talks about her experiences making more than 300 successful ascents up some of the world's loftiest mountains. Her accomplishments range from the first all-woman climb to the top of Denali, the American Bicentennial Everest Expedition, as well as a 2,400-mile trek across Bhutan, Nepal and India. As I read Blum's story, I was struck by her final insight. Describing a successful and meaningful climb, she discusses the hardest, but most important challenge of the journey – *the last 5%.* She says:

In so many of the things we do in life – from projects at work to household chores to climbing a mountain – we find reasons not to do the last 5%. With a Himalayan expedition, you spend years raising funds, you travel all the way to Nepal, you carry loads between camps for six weeks. Then, finally, it's summit day and you're hours from the top – but it's too cold, it's too steep or you're too tired.

I've been so successful in my climbing because I usually haven't turned back during that final, exhausting 5%. Making it to the top isn't about the final sprint; it's about maintaining your rhythm – even if that rhythm is five breaths for every one step. That kind of focus means that you're more likely to have the energy to deal with unforeseen challenges – and less likely to lose sight of why you're climbing the mountain in the first place.[2]

Five breaths per step – sometimes that's how it feels when we're reaching for a goal. But Blum's discipline is key. She didn't give up or turn back. Perhaps she wondered what on earth she was climbing the mountain for, as many of us do when we hit obstacles in our lives, but she took the five breaths and kept going.

Passion, knowledge, hope, focus, strategy, faith and initiative are the essential components to foster creativity, productivity and enjoyment in the midst of change.

[2] *Fast Company, "Here's How to Make It To the Top",
Arlene Blum, September 1998, p. 74*

- ◆ Knowledge determines hope.
- ◆ Hope without knowledge is only a dream.
- ◆ Faith without knowledge is merely presumption.
- ◆ Action without knowledge, hope and faith is misguided and pointless.

Think about each of these elements when you face any new piece of music in your personal or professional life.

Putting All the Pieces Together

We've come to the end of this book. I hope you've learned a few important principles and have been inspired to face your unknown future in an optimistic way. Perhaps you have been challenged to take the leap and start a journey that you have been contemplating for some time. Or, perhaps you have been encouraged to explore some familiar ideas in a new way – after all, that is what transitional living is all about.

In the Fall of 1998, I was speaking at the National Recreational Vehicle Convention in Orlando, Florida. Since Susie and I had never been in Orlando before, we went together and stayed for the weekend to visit the Kennedy Space Center. As we toured around, we were overwhelmed by the many dreams that had come true. In 1962, the space race to the moon seemed like an impossibility. With President Kennedy's assassination and the many failures and setbacks to the Apollo moon projects, it seemed that the United States would never accomplish President Kennedy's goal of putting a man on the moon and bringing him home safely before the end of the decade. But they did.

Although this book is primarily about managing transitions, it is also a book about dreams. As you go back and review the 8 essential strategies to facing change, notice how each one of them is connected to our dreams.

Essential One: Discover Your Passion
♦   Passion is the energy of the dream.

Essential Two: Visualize Your Hope
♦   Hope is the object of the dream.

Essential Three: Manage the Culture Shock of the Transitional Stages
♦   The transitional stages are the testing ground of the dream.

Essential Four: Leverage Your Value with Intellectual Capital
♦   Knowledge is the foundation of the dream.

Essential Five: Focus Your Dream
♦   Focus is the power of the dream.

Essential Six: Think Strategically
♦   Strategic thinking identifies the CSF's to accomplish the dream.

Essential Seven: Keep the Faith
♦   Faith is the antidote for dream doubt.

Essential Eight: Just Do It!
♦   Action is the proof of a dream's passion, hope, knowledge, focus, strategy and faith.

A Final Call

This raises one final challenge I want to leave with you. Each chapter of this book outlines one strategic essential that is merely one rung on the ladder of success. Many people have taken the first step and then stop. But with every additional step you take, you enhance the value of your first step. Success is the sum of small efforts repeated day in and day out.

Little of what I have presented here falls into the "instant cure" category. All of these ideas require attention to detail and commitment to work. However, I do believe that they are not overwhelming. We can create a new future and learn to live life in the expectation that no matter what kind of change, no matter what kind of music is placed before us, we can pick up the baton of personal leadership and face the unknown with confidence and hope.

God bless you in your new future.

Thomas McKee

Appendix

Developing Your New
Future Mission Statement

Step One:

Answer these questions in ten words of less

What are you?
> Use some adjectives to describe you.

What do you do?
> What are the tasks you will do that highly energize you?

Who is your customer?
> Who is going to benefit from your tasks?

What impact do I have on my customers?
> How will your customers benefit from your skills?

What makes you unique?
> What do you have to offer your customers that others offering this service do not have?

How do you market this service?
> How can you get this message out to the people who need to hear your message?

Step Two:

Take the answers from the above questions and develop them into a two or three sentence mission statement for your new future.

Visioning Your Dream

1. Take thirty uninterrupted minutes and write down at
    least 30 things that you want to do before you die.
    Try for 50 if you can. Think of educational desires,
    physical, vocational, recreational, spiritual, financial,
    family, etc.

2. Pick the top five and prioritize them.

3. Place a "$" by each one that will cost money to
    accomplish. Ask how much.

4. Place an "S" (to indicate support) by each one in
    which you feel you have the encouragement and
    support from the significant people in your life
    (spouse, family, friends, etc.).

Place a "V" by any of them that are visionary in your
estimation.

Develop Your Strategic Plan

The following outline is a suggested agenda of questions for a personal strategic retreat. Spend a half-day, day or weekend working through the following questions:

I. Where am I?
 SWOT analysis (Strengths, Weaknesses, Opportunities, Threats)
(See Next Page)
   Internal analysis: Those factors that relate to who and what I am?
                What are my most significant strengths?
                What are my most significant weaknesses?
   External analysis: Those factors that go beyond my direct influence
                What are my opportunities?
                What are my threats?
   Values: What do I value?

II.   Where do I want to be?
   What is my personal mission (appendix page 118)
   What is my vision (appendix page 119)
   What one word factors will affect accomplishing my vision?
   Which of these factors do I have complete control, indirect
   control and no control?

III. What is the gap? The Critical Success Factors (CSF)
         What are the factors that are critical to fill the gap between
         where I am and where I want to be?
 ♦ Each CSF must be necessary.
 ♦ Begin each CSF with "I must"
 ♦ Altogether, the CSF's must be sufficient to accomplish your vision.
 ♦ CSF's are statements of hope (goals), not how.
 ♦ Each CSF focuses on one thing.
         There should be at least four and no more than eight CSF's
         (more then eight becomes too overwhelming).

SWOT Analysis

In the following chart, fill out the individual sections starting with the internal analysis. List your strengths and weaknesses in the appropriate box. Do the same in the external analysis section and list your opportunities and threats.

	Strengths	**Weaknesses**
Internal Analysis		
External Analysis	**Opportunities**	**Threats**

About Advantage Point Systems, Inc.
Gaining the tools, confidence and hope to face an unknown future.

Advantage Point Systems, Inc. is a staff development and human resource company. Our staff is dedicated to helping you and your staff manage the transitions of doing business. We have developed a unique system to help you build synergistic teams during unremitting transitions.

Our Mission
Our mission is to help you, your business or your organization position itself for growth and success during transitional times.

Our Meaning
Ad-van-tage: any state or opportunity favorable to success

Point: a critical position in the course of affairs

Systems: the mechanism to make it work

Our Services
Transition workshops and motivational sessions
- How to Make the Team Work During Transition
- Just When I Learned to Speak, People Quit Listening (communication during times of transition)
- Some Cats Got It, Some Cats Don't (effective sales during times of transition)
- Customer Service is Not a Department (Cus-

tomer service is an attitude of generosity that transforms an organization)
♦   Stress Busters (managing stress during transition)
♦   New Supervisor and Manager Training (making the transition to supervision)
♦   Fight or Flight (conflict resolution and transition)

Strategic Retreats
♦   Transition time boot camps
♦   Strategic planning retreats

For more information:
    Advantage Point Systems, Inc.
    11857 Old Eureka Way
    Gold River, CA 95670 U.S.A.
    (916) 635-9677
    (800) 366-3061
    www.advantagepoint.com

Order Form

Fax Orders: (916) 635-6184
Telephone Orders: Call toll-free: 1 (800) 366-3061
On-line Orders: http://www.advantagepoint.com
Postal Orders: Advantage Point Systems, Inc.
                      11857 Old Eureka Way
                      Gold River, CA 95670 U.S.A.

Please send me the following books: I understand that I may return any books for a full refund for any reason.

_____

_____

Company Name: _____

Name: _____

Address: _____

City: _____ State: _____ Zip: _____

Telephone: (_____) _____

Email: _____

Sales Tax: Please add 7.75% for books shipped within California
Shipping: $4.00 for the first book and $2.00 for each additional one.
Payment: ____Check _____Credit Card
Type of Card (circle one): Visa   Mastercard

Card Number:_____

Name on Card:_____Exp Date___ / ___

Order Form

Fax Orders: (916) 635-6184
Telephone Orders: Call toll-free: 1 (800) 366-3061
On-line Orders: http://www.advantagepoint.com
Postal Orders: Advantage Point Systems, Inc.
                     11857 Old Eureka Way
                     Gold River, CA 95670 U.S.A.

Please send me the following books: I understand that I may return any books for a full refund for any reason.

_____

_____

Company Name: _____

Name: _____

Address: _____

City: _____ State: _____ Zip: _____

Telephone: (_____) _____

Email: _____

Sales Tax: Please add 7.75% for books shipped within California
Shipping: $4.00 for the first book and $2.00 for each additional one.
Payment: _____Check _____Credit Card
Type of Card (circle one): Visa   Mastercard

Card Number:_____

Name on Card:_____ Exp Date___/___